The Woman's Book
of Confidence

The Woman's Book of Confidence

Meditations for Strength & Inspiration

SUE PATTON THOELE

MJF BOOKS
NEW YORK

Published by MJF Books
Fine Communications
Two Lincoln Square
60 West 66th Street
New York, NY 10023

The Woman's Book of Confidence
Library of Congress Catalog Card Number 98-67586
ISBN 1-56731-301-9

Copyright © 1992, 1997 by Sue Patton Thoele
Cover Design: Leigh Wells
Cover Illustration: Rae Ecklund
Author photo: Paige Eden Thoele
This edition published by arrangement with Conari Press.

10   9   8   7   6   5   4   3   2

Dedication

Especially for Gene, my husband
and greatest supporter.
And to our children,
Paige, Brett, Mike, and Lynnie,
our son-in-love, Shawn,
and our grandson, Joshua,
who have blessed our lives immeasurably.
Also to the sister of my soul,
Bonnie Hampton.

Acknowledgments

First I would like to express my gratitude to the unseen supporters whom I feel standing beside me as I write, encouraging me to keep on keeping on. I would like to thank all the wonderful people at Conari Press and especially my editor, Mary Jane, whose gentle guidance and trust in me makes the writing process a joy and a privilege. I am so grateful to Gene, my best friend, for his unfailing support and much needed hugs, especially when the computer-Genie begins pulling his nefarious tricks.

The friends and family members from whom I receive support and love are too numerous to mention, but you know who you are, and I hope you also know how much I love and appreciate you!

For the insights they have provided, I also wish to thank each of the writers whose words I have quoted. And a special thank-you to all the women whose stories I have shared in these pages. Your journeys toward enduring self-confidence, trust, and acceptance are a constant source of awe and inspiration to me.

Contents

Introduction

Having confidence in ourselves is essential if we're to make our lives what we want and deserve them to be. But there are many day-to-day influences that can drain our confidence. When we take a realistic look at the booby traps our society sets for women's self-esteem, is it any wonder that many of us experience confidence crises regularly? In the four years since *The Woman's Book of Confidence* was first published, I've been appalled by the way we women have been continually brainwashed by the unrealistic expectations about what it takes to be good-looking, intelligent, and happy. To say nothing of sexy, successful, and a super-mom.

Most of us can never be as skinny or as physically fit as the models touted as the ideal of feminine beauty whom we see in print or on television. In actuality, most of us wouldn't be healthy if we could whittle ourselves to their size. And, it turns out, neither are they. Recently, thank goodness, there has been some honest reporting about the beauty industry and the battles that many of the models have gone through, including bulimia and anorexia, in their quest for acceptance and success in their field.

We, too, yearn for acceptance in our lives and the margins of acceptable parameters seem to be shrinking. Not only beauty, but behavior, intelligence, success, popularity, and mothering, to name only a few criteria, are being measured by an ever narrowing yardstick. We are our own harshest judges, and I'm overwhelmingly sad to say that especially young girls, even preteens, are now becoming afflicted with the impossible mission of perfection as put forth by the entertainment and advertising worlds. No wonder we sometimes feel as insignificant as a ladybug at the base of the Great Wall of China. We must, and we can, change the trend toward impossible perfection.

We need to learn to turn a deaf ear and a blind eye toward the ridiculous injunctions about what beauty, intelligence, or success is and create our own yardstick based on our unique individual aspirations, talents, and— very importantly—also our limitations. We women and girls are inherently darned fabulous no matter what size our bodies or our brains are because most of us have gigantic hearts, and that is what's important. We need to give ourselves a break, and having confidence is a key to doing this.

We're going to need to help each other because, although women find it easy to believe in other people's talents, abilities, and basic goodness, they often have difficulty believing in their own. Generally we are very gifted at instilling confidence in others, but often find it a challenge to maintain a firm sense of self-confidence. We're quick to unselfishly comfort and inspire friends or family members who are thrashing around under the heel of unrealistic expectations or in physical or emotional pain, but, unfortunately, we're often equally quick to chastise or criticize ourselves for feeling or acting less than completely wonderful. Frequently, we offer solace to others but only censure to ourselves.

The habit of undermining our self-confidence by being hard on ourselves comes from various sources besides Hollywood and its cohorts. One possibility is that we didn't receive the kind and amount of support and encouragement we needed as we were growing up and therefore think we don't deserve it now. Another is the belief that we deserve to be ruled by a relentless taskmaster; for some unknown reason we're not as good as we should be, we don't measure up—and, therefore, earn our own criticism.

Neither assumption is healthy or confidence

building. It's also very likely that neither is true. In the course of my life and career I've met thousands of women; not only are the vast majority of them lovingly—even heroically—dealing with their lives in the best way they know how, but they are constantly looking for ways to do a better job. They, and we all, deserve and need the comfort of self-acceptance and understanding, not the discouragement of disapproval and condemnation.

Mastering the art of emotionally supporting ourselves through self-acceptance and encouragement can lead to a deep inner friendship which, in turn, builds confidence. We can liken such a friendship to a greenhouse in which delicate seedlings are given the best environment possible to foster growth. In the tender and gentle atmosphere of a nurturing greenhouse, plants and flowers mature into their natural beauty. So, too, can the Self flourish with our gentle and loving care.

If the emotional greenhouse we have been providing for ourselves doesn't sustain us in difficult times and enhance our lives in good times, we can change it. We can learn to give ourselves a comforting climate of genuine self-love and acceptance, one that enhances confidence by inspiring us to blossom into our vast potential for wisdom, beauty, and service.

It is my wish that *The Woman's Book of Confidence* becomes a gentle greenhouse for you, a quiet place in which you can learn to compassionately befriend and trust yourself. I hope that the true stories and meditations in these pages act as little buds of encouragement, comfort, and inspiration, helping you have confidence in yourself just as you are now, not as you wish you were or as they think you should be. As I know it is for many of us, gaining and sustaining self-confidence has been a continuing struggle for me. Only through learning to consistently treat myself lovingly have I been able to maintain a sense of enduring self-worth. Feelings of worthiness inevitably enhance confidence. Even though they are often hard to do, guided meditations and affirmations—such as those found in *The Woman's Book of Confidence*—are very effective instruments for pulling us out of the black pit of low self-esteem.

There are many ways to utilize *The Woman's Book of Confidence*. It can be used as a self-discovery guide by reading one section and chronicling what you discover about yourself in a personal journal until you feel complete with what that particular section has to offer. Or you may want to look in the Table of Contents and allow yourself to be guided to the entry that "speaks to you" on a day-by-day basis. (One reader told me that she takes the opportunity to give herself a gold star when coming to a section that she feels she already does a good job with. Gold stars are confidence-creators. Good greenhouses are filled with them!)

Using the book's ideas and meditations in a supportive group setting is another valuable way to encourage personal growth. Intimately and honestly sharing experiences and feelings with other women can foster tremendous leaps in self-confidence and create healing at the very depths of our being.

Developing interior intimacy by becoming our own trustworthy and caring friend generates a wellspring of security within us. Our ability to open our hearts to others flows from the security we unstintingly create for ourselves. Thus the capacity to emotionally comfort and support ourselves endows us with the desire and the energy to love and serve others from a sense of personal overflow rather than obligation. Focusing on ourselves with encouragement and support may seem selfish to us, but it isn't. If we're to lighten the burden of our children, sisters and brothers, and our planet, we need to first lighten our own load by mending our personal brokenness. Love and acceptance are the best healers there are.

When we have the courage to gently mine the vast wealth of our interior selves, we will discover that it is absolutely possible to trust our innate wisdom and goodness. From a heart overflowing with self-respect and acceptance, we can more readily comfort, support, and accept others. Let there be peace on Mother Earth, and let it begin in our own hearts.

Weaving a Safety Net

Woman must not depend upon the protection of man, but must be taught to protect herself.

—Susan Brownell Anthony

WOMEN ARE AMAZING. OUR lives are rarely a straight trajectory; instead we weave together an abundant existence from the varied and often unexpected occurrences that we encounter. Sociologists claim that women, because they are required to pay attention to many things at once, are *multiple-minded* and have great tolerance for interruption. Anyone who has juggled motherhood, career, education, myriad significant relationships, household management, and self-growth knows this to be true.

As we handle the woof and warp of our diverse lives, we need to be sure we weave strong safety nets for ourselves. When demands on us exceed our energy, we need to know how to support ourselves in finding the rejuvenation necessary to continue to thrive.

There are many ways—such as learning to understand and honor our needs, having realistic expectations, asking for help, and abolishing guilt—by which we can weave a supportive safety net for ourselves. I hope the following section provides you with strong fibers you can use to design a durable net that will comfort and support you when you need it.

Sharing Roots

ON A TRIP UP THE COAST OF CALIFORNIA and Oregon, I learned a valuable lesson about mutual support from the majestic redwood trees thriving there. Redwoods are inclusive beings—as they grow they incorporate into their basic structure objects around them, including rocks and other trees. Although redwoods have shallow roots they are noted for their strength and longevity because they share their roots with others. Each individual tree is invited into the whole and, in turn, helps support the entire group. This adaptation appears to have worked, for redwoods are among the oldest living things on earth.

Feminine energy is naturally inclusive and in order to survive and thrive we, too, need to learn to consciously share our roots with others, to ask for encouragement and support when we need it, and stand ready to give the same to those who come to us.

Eve, a single mother, was struggling with the idea of returning to graduate school. For weeks she kept her questions to herself for fear of appearing immature and needy. But when she finally risked talking to several women who had gone back to school, she was encouraged and supported by them. They included her in their root system. As a result of their discussions she began to feel clear about her next step. By having the courage to ask for help, Eve not only ended her confusion but found a support group that understood her circumstances.

In the process of creating support systems we need to be sure that those with whom we choose to share our feelings can be trusted to honor them. The best way to ascertain the trustworthiness of others is by monitoring your feelings as you talk to them. If you feel safe and understood, you have probably found a grove of like-minded redwoods.

By sharing our roots of compassion and support, we women, like the redwoods, create a safety net in which the whole is greater than the sum of its parts.

*I have the courage to ask for support
when I need it.*

*I am willing to support others
when they need my help.*

Editing Out Guilt

WOMEN ARE OFTEN PLAGUED BY FEELINGS of guilt, but I learned an interesting thing recently: guilt is a strictly English word. No other Germanic or Indo-European language has it. We need to follow the lead of these other cultures and edit the word guilt—and guilt feelings—out of our lives.

Feeling guilty drains our confidence and becomes a habit if we have been conditioned to be overly responsible for our own and others' behaviors and attitudes. Millie, a client in her mid-fifties, came to see me because she felt depressed most of the time. As we talked it became apparent that Millie was a Responsibility Sponge who sopped up everyone's messes. While discussing her unemployed thirty-year-old son, Millie sighed repeatedly and finally said, "I wonder where I failed?" When I asked her why it was her fault her son was not working, she looked at me with surprise and said, "Well, because I'm his mother."

Exploring Millie's background uncovered a family structure built on guilt and shame. Because of her conditioning, Millie got in the habit of assuming responsibility for everything and everyone around her. Since she, like the rest of us, had no real power over anyone's actions but her own, she felt discouraged and depressed. Millie decided to edit guilt out of her life using the following technique.

When you begin to experience guilt, ask yourself these questions: What have I really done to feel guilty about? (If there is something specific, decide whether you can rectify it, and if so, how.) Why am I responsible for this? Does this feeling and circumstance remind me of a pattern in my family? Do I want to keep feeling guilty about this?

If the answer to the last question is no, take a sheet of paper and write down what you feel guilty about. Now, with the biggest, reddest marker you can find, cross it out—delete it. If you find yourself still mired in guilt, remind yourself: *Guilt is a word and feeling I am editing out of my life!*

*I give myself permission to erase
guilt from my vocabulary and my life.*

*I have the courage to accept
responsibility appropriately.*

Coping Creatively

ALL OF US HAVE OUR OWN STYLE FOR coping creatively. Some of us, like me, talk out our difficulties and, in the process of speaking the words, are able to work through the situation and resultant feelings. Others feel better able to sort through and arrive at solutions by mulling things over privately. Very often people in close relationships cope differently, and this can make each partner feel that she or he is doing it wrong. At such times, we need to remember that so long as we do so constructively, we each have the right to move through our problems in a way that is natural for us.

When Blair is confused or hurt, she needs to talk things through in order to gain a healthy perspective on her predicament, but her dear friend Marilyn is a solo-solution person. Blair used to chop holes in her personal safety net by comparing her style of coping with Marilyn's. She told herself that Marilyn was strong whereas she was a weak whiner, and that her friend must be smarter and healthier since she didn't seem to need help working things out. Most important, Blair was afraid Marilyn was tired of hearing her talk and was disgusted with her.

I suggested Blair start honoring her own style by talking out her feelings with Marilyn. When she did, Blair found that Marilyn accepted and enjoyed her need to talk—that Marilyn actually took into the privacy of her own process what she learned from their discussions and it often helped her heal more quickly.

It is important that we emotionally support ourselves by accepting and trusting our individual coping style, realizing that although there is no one right way, there is *our* way, and we need to honor it.

I have confidence in my ability to cope creatively with my challenges.

I recognize and honor my own style of working things through.

I have a right to my unique style of coping.

Pampering Is Permissible

WHEN I ASK WOMEN CLIENTS WHO SEEM drained what they do to pamper themselves, many of them respond uncomprehendingly, as though I've just spoken in a foreign language. To most of us, pampering brings to mind diapers or what we do for others. The idea of indulging ourselves is an alien concept; if it does occur, we avoid the idea because it smacks of being spoiled or selfish. After all, we've been taught to be givers rather than receivers.

Sarah, a workaholic, was married to a man who was still a little boy in terms of accepting responsibility at home. By the time she sought counseling, Sarah was, in her terms, "a raving, ranting bitch." Her bitchiness came from her anger at being the only adult in the family shouldering career, housework, and childcare. In the process of attempting to change her husband, Sarah had totally neglected herself and her emotional safety net was virtually nonexistent. Her nerves were frayed to the breaking point and she was lashing out in frustration.

I encouraged her to stop working so hard for him and start taking care of herself and then both of them might learn to believe that she was worth taking care of. It was very difficult for Sarah to change, but she began with the small step of allowing herself one hour a week just for the "luxury" of what she wanted to do.

Eventually she realized that she was not only more confident and rested but also a better parent, worker, and wife when she pampered herself a little each day. She is now able to care for herself in small ways, such as saying no when she feels like it, and large ways such as taking a trip she has set aside money for. Her children adapted quickly and have accepted and learned from their mother's ability to take care of herself. Even her husband is changing a little. Most important, Sarah is happier and healthier.

Weave a pampering pattern into your safety net. Make a list of ways in which you would like to pamper yourself, and then, starting with small steps, indulge yourself. You'll be better for it!

❀

I have the courage to pamper myself.

I am worthy of receiving as well as giving.

Pampering and taking care of myself is a heal thy thing to do.

Heeding Physical Clues

RUTH, A SOCIAL WORKER, TRIED TO ignore the illnesses her body was experiencing. From her training, she knew that there was probably a psychological reason for her recurring ill health, but the thought of searching for the cause frightened her so much she chose to deny her body's signals. It was only after two near death experiences and many years of pain and frustration that Ruth realized that if she wanted to live she had to look at what her body was trying to tell her.

Although always a very private person, Ruth gave herself permission to reach out to a few friends and family members for support and encouragement as she courageously began to explore her hidden emotional pain. The root of her ill health turned out to be her despair over her emotionally imbalanced marriage. Since facing those feelings and addressing them creatively, Ruth's health has returned to almost normal.

We can have confidence that our bodies have been given to us as miraculous vehicles for our consciousness, and it is our sacred duty to appreciate and care for them. No one but ourselves is privileged to the information our body gives us. Only we can weave a safety net of personal health and well-being by heeding the clues of our wise and deserving body.

Sit quietly with your eyes closed and thank your body for its wisdom and the faithful way it serves you. Gently bless your body, especially any part feeling discomfort. With as much acceptance as you can, focus your attention on any pain or illness you are experiencing and ask your body what you need to do to help alleviate the discomfort. Open your heart and mind to recognizing and acting on the clues your body is giving you.

I encourage my body by listening to its wisdom.

I honor and care for my wondrous body by recognizing the clues it gives me.

I have the courage to explore the psychological causes of my illnesses.

Softening Our Perfectionist

THE TROUBLE WITH BEING A PERFECTIONIST is that anything less than perfection displeases us. Since life is only sprinkled with perfect, fairy-dust moments while swamped with average-to-mediocre times, a perfectionist is only momentarily happy, which results in a pretty tedious life.

As for being a perfect person, having a perfect relationship, or doing all things perfectly, *there ain't no such thing!* And recognizing this increases our day-to-day happiness.

I used to have a part of myself that I named Ms. Perfection. When I visualized her, she was tall, bony, and ramrod straight with her hair pulled severely back into a knot. She wore half-glasses, a serviceable sweater with patches at the elbows, and white gloves with which she tested my ability to keep a sparkling house and personality. She made my life miserable until I learned to soften her by getting to know her and finding out what she needed from me.

As I became acquainted with Ms. Perfection, I became aware of her feeling that she was the only one of my inner cast of characters who acted responsibly. She believed she had to shoulder the adult stuff all alone and, therefore, had no choice but to be a rigid and harsh taskmaster. What she needed from me was a more consistent sense of responsibility and maturity. As I began working on that, she relaxed somewhat and became less judgmental.

Become aware of your perfectionist and ask yourself these questions: What does my perfectionist look like? Why does she act the way she does? What is she afraid of? What does she need from me? Am I willing to get to know this part of myself and help transform her by giving her what she needs, within reason?

Softening our perfectionist helps weave a safety net free from the gaping holes of impossible demands.

❧

*I have the right and responsibility to soften
my perfectionist.*

I am worthwhile even though imperfect.

I loosen up and enjoy life's little imperfections.

Excusing Is Often Inexcusable

TO ENJOY INTIMATE AND AUTHENTIC relationships, we must be able to understand and forgive ourselves and others. But we women sometimes confuse *excusing* with understanding and forgiving. Excusing, a codependent and childish habit, is the first cousin of denial. Excusing ourselves and others lets us off the hook by not addressing the consequences or responsibilities of our behavior. Alcoholic families frequently pivot around excuses.

Inherent in the process of excusing is our willingness to take responsibility for the actions of others. Continually excusing unacceptable actions does not create a climate that fosters growth and learning, in fact it can be an implied put-down. When we excuse the inexcusable, we are subtly saying that the person who is excused is not capable of right behavior.

On the other hand, understanding is a strong strand in our emotional safety net. Understanding our own and others' actions and attitudes provides an honest framework in which we can create an atmosphere of acceptance and forgiveness—an environment in which people and relationships can mature and thrive.

Understanding requires commitment, energy, and the willingness to be with ourselves and others in a heartfelt and open way. We need to make the effort to search for the causes and motives behind our own negative behaviors or attitudes and do what is necessary to heal them. Of course we can't do that for others, but we can tell them when their behavior is unacceptable to us and gently remove ourselves from their presence. Excusing may be initially more effortless than awareness, but it does not lead to intimacy, honesty, or authenticity.

I give up excusing my own and others' actions.

I want to understand myself and others.

I open myself to the ability to understand and forgive.

Gathering Ourselves Together

HAVE YOU EVER SAID, "I'M JUST BESIDE myself today!"? Our lives are often like fall storms whipping branches and flinging the leaves of our concentration and contentment to the four winds, causing us to wonder how we can keep on keeping on. When we feel fragmented, we are actually beside ourselves energetically and need to gather ourselves back together again.

My wise mentor, Annabelle, taught me the following meditation that brings me immeasurable comfort when I feel frazzled and frayed. The purpose is to align our physical, emotional, and mental elements under our Higher Selves, which moves us from feeling beside ourselves to being integrated.

Close your eyes and visualize your physical, emotional, and mental selves. They can appear in any form or you may merely sense them. If you're feeling chaotic, they may appear to be moving quickly and, possibly, swirling out of control. After you see or sense these three aspects of yourself, envision your Higher Self— your spiritual part—above the other three. Softly say, "Together, together, together," three times—a total of nine *togethers*. As you repeat the words, picture the symbols for your physical, emotional, and mental aspects gathering together under, and finally into, your spiritual part. As you visualize, gently repeat the series of nine *togethers* until the parts merge and you begin to feel a sense of calm replacing the chaos.

Even though this exercise may seem simplistic, it speaks powerfully to our subconscious mind and allows us to gather our energy together, thereby naturally balancing and harmonizing our feelings. Standing in our own skins, rather than being "beside ourselves" allows us to move constructively through our busy lives, feeling *in sync*.

❧

I have the power to replace chaos with calm.

I balance and harmonize the four aspects of my being.

Greeting the Stranger
Who Is Myself

WOMEN HAVE ALWAYS KNOWN THE importance of networking with other women, and now, because we travel the career path as well as the family path, we are also recognizing the value of networking within our chosen field. We go to meetings and join clubs for the express purpose of meeting people we can assist and be assisted by. But how many strangers are waiting inside of us for encouragement, acceptance, and support?

Kathleen was so sick of her job that she woke every Monday morning with a severe headache. Sometimes she burst into tears at the sound of the alarm. Even with messages as strong as these, she continued to work at the hated place. When I asked her why, she said she believed she would never find a superior job so she had better stay put. Another voice in her head told her she was darn lucky just to have work. And deeply buried was a barely audible, tiny little voice telling her she didn't deserve to be happy so it was fitting that she had a job that made her unhappy.

Courageously Kathleen began to greet these inner strangers. She found that many of the *shoulds* and *have to's* they spoke echoed what she had been taught as a young, single mother, having to work to support herself and her child. But the most important voice she became acquainted with was the tiny little girl inside who knew she didn't deserve happiness.

Kathleen made a commitment to comfort that little person who believed she was bad because she had never been able to please her critical and unloving mother. As her internal little girl became more secure and confident, Kathleen's sense of herself as a deserving person expanded. I am happy to say that she is now updating her resume, actively researching other work opportunities, and feeling vastly relieved.

Before she could successfully network in her workplace, Kathleen had to network within herself. Understanding and accepting the strangers within us provides an underlying strength to our emotional safety nets.

❦

I listen to the voices of my inner selves.
I love and accept all of myself.

Growing a Tail

IT IS VERY IMPORTANT FOR US TO LEARN to ask for help and be willing to receive it, but it's even more important that we learn how to help ourselves. We're our constant companion and we know, better than anyone else, what is good for us and what we want and need.

The phrase, "God helps those who help themselves" is a sound and practical philosophy and one we would do well to follow. But I also love the lighter approach taken by the African proverb, "God will not drive flies away from a tailless cow." We all know tailless cows, people who always look outside of themselves for solutions and are adept at never taking responsibility for their own lives. Tiresome, aren't they!

During the trauma of the breakup of my first marriage, I regressed to a helpless state in which I, at first of necessity and then out of habit, hung on to my friends for support while consistently lamenting my situation. They were patiently willing to be there for me for quite a while, but finally my tailless state caused one friend to confront me about my seeming inability to help myself. Although the confrontation was extremely painful for me, it opened my eyes and I began to accept responsibility for my part in the breakup and learn ways to take charge of my own life. I grew a tail. At first it was neither a handsome nor effective tail, but it grew into a much stronger "fly foe" with practice.

Being able to rely on ourself as a loving helpmate is an integral part of weaving a powerful safety net. As we learn to consistently trust and support ourselves, our tails lengthen and, sometimes, some of the flies that have been persistently pestering us become discouraged and disappear altogether.

I am willing and able to help myself.

I take responsibility for my actions and reactions.

I have a long, strong tail for brushing away the annoying flies of life.

Swimming in Buoyant Waters

ONCE, ON THE WAY HOME FROM California, my son and I drove through Salt Lake City. Remembering the strange experience of swimming in the Great Salt Lake when I was a kid, I asked Brett if he'd like to stop and try it. "Mom, I sink like a rock every time I try to float!" he answered. "You won't here," I promised him. And of course he didn't, because the Great Salt Lake assists even the most leaden among us to float effortlessly.

A big help in establishing a safety net is finding buoyant emotional waters that can support us when we feel in danger of drowning. It is essential that we create an atmosphere around us that helps us stay on top of the water rather than thrash and struggle through it.

How do we do this? Choosing to be around people who are up-lifters, rather than weights around our necks, is a very crucial part of establishing an environment that helps keep us afloat. *Up-lift* people accept us as we are and are truly interested in us. They are kind and do not put us down or demean us in any way. In their presence we feel good.

Of course, it's essential that our internal voices are up-lifters also, that we speak to ourselves in supportive and encouraging ways, because even surrounded by the most buoyant people, if we still speak to ourselves in a concrete-shoe way, we will sink.

Ours is the one ever-present voice in our lives. Therefore, it is crucial that our self-talk instill confidence within us and is supportive, not submerging, and that our attitudes toward ourselves help keep our spirits afloat through acceptance and trust. We are our own most important and influential buoy.

❧

I buoy up my spirits with positive self-talk.

I deserve to be surrounded by people who support and accept me.

I search out environments in which it is possible for me to float.

Walking in Another's Shoes

EVERYONE HAS PEBBLES IN THEIR moccasins. In order to understand someone else we need to walk in her shoes—exchange our point of view for hers—for a little while. Doing this will allow us to let go of critical attitudes toward her. Of course, there are people with whom we will never feel compatible or want to cultivate a friendship, but we can coexist better by taking the time to try and understand their perspective.

Bertie's daughter-in-law, Tina, successfully tried to separate her from her son and grand-daughter, and Bertie couldn't understand why. Being very conscious of mother-in-law jokes and pitfalls, she had tried to be caring but unobtrusive toward her son's family. She spent many fruitless hours lying awake fuming at Tina's actions, wondering how she could change her, until finally she exchanged her resistance for a desire to understand her better. Bertie made a choice to listen with her heart as well as her ears.

From the few fragments Tina was willing to share, Bertie pieced together an awareness of her daughter-in-law's fear of being controlled.

Her new found awareness allowed Bertie to re-alize *she wasn't doing anything wrong* and to com-passionately stop resisting Tina's choices. While it didn't change Tina's behavior, it did give Bertie much greater peace of mind.

Take a moment to imagine yourself in the symbolic shoes of someone with whom you have difficulty. Visualize how those shoes fit and feel. Do they pinch? Are they awkwardly large? Filled with grit? Allow yourself to really absorb what it must be like to walk in these par-ticular moccasins. What do you now under-stand about this person?

Although we can't always alter circum-stances, we can always transform how we per-ceive them. As we move from criticism and judgment to acceptance and understanding, our personal safety net is reinforced.

I take the time to listen to myself and others in order to better understand.

If I feel judgmental toward someone, I walk in their shoes for a moment.

Finding a Hand Up
When We Bottom Out

THERE ARE TIMES IN EACH OF OUR LIVES when it feels as though the pins have been kicked out from under us and we're absolutely sure we've bottomed out. Some of us feel guilty if we can't go it alone during such difficult times. But it's often healthier for us to ask for a hand up when we find ourselves in the pits. Trying to deal with things totally alone can magnify our pain and lead to feelings of depression and isolation.

Susan's husband was experiencing physical symptoms that doctors feared were indicative of a brain tumor. His way of coping was to deal with the physical pain moment by moment but not talk about the illness until he knew for sure what it was. He didn't want other people to know because "they would worry, and couldn't do anything anyway." Susan, who was beside herself with worry, felt more comforted when she was able to talk through her emotions with a select group of friends.

Although her husband objected to her sharing her fears at first, Susan convinced him that she had the right, and the need, to cope in her way just as he did in his. Only after she reached out to her friends did Susan feel able to climb out of her crater of despair and begin to draw on the strength she inherently possessed.

The story has a happy ending. Susan's husband's illness was treated successfully, and in spite of his original protests, she had the courage to comfort herself by honoring her need to reach out for solace and support.

If you are grieving or in pain, ask yourself if you are gritting your teeth and trying to handle the situation all by yourself when you might feel better reaching out. Or have you clenched your fists in anger and defiance at your misfortune and, consequently, could not accept a helping hand even if it were offered? If finding a hand up when you bottom out creates a secure and comforting safety net for you, give yourself permission to ask for help when you need it.

❦

I honor what I want and need when I'm in crisis.

I am able to reach out to others for help.

I allow others to give me a hand up.

Acting As the Arms of God

ACTING AS THE ARMS OF GOD BY OPENING ourselves to service for others is a beautiful pattern we women weave into our safety nets. Lending a hand and an empathetic ear can be a tremendous heart-lift not only to the person in need but also to the person serving. By opening ourselves to the needs of others we often find that we are "in the flow" where opportunities to be helpful present themselves in the most serendipitous ways.

One of my favorite stories about being given the opportunity to act as God's arms and help someone concerns Carole, a social worker. She and her husband were waiting for a table in a restaurant called Friends & Company when she noticed the hostess struggling with a phone call. Finally the hostess turned to the waiting customers and said frantically, "I've got a woman on the line who is hysterical and I just can't hang up on her. Is there anyone here who can help?"

Carole agreed to take the call and talked to the distraught woman for half an hour. She was able not only to calm the caller but also to offer practical advice about where she could turn for long-term help. The woman had called the restaurant because all she could think to do in her distressed state of mind was to look in the phone book under *Friend*.

When we commit ourselves to supporting and comforting ourselves by becoming our own good friend, a natural outcome will be the desire to recycle support by befriending others. The most important door we can open in our desire to be service-full is the one to our own hearts. Loving and accepting ourselves in a genuinely *heart-felt* way opens our hearts to others as well and invites God to use us as She sees fit.

I support myself and, in turn, am happy
to support others.

I open myself to being service-full.

I welcome opportunities to act as the arms of God.

Creating a Safe House

IN RECENT YEARS OUR SOCIETY HAS established "safe houses" where battered women and children can find shelter. These secure havens are available only to the severely abused, however, so what about those of us who don't feel emotionally safe in our own homes or workplaces? If we are experiencing unacceptable behavior directed toward us by others, we need to set limits and clearly express what we will and will not tolerate so far as other people's attitudes and behavior go.

Although Sammi was highly respected in the business community, in her own home she experienced only resistance and rebellion from her kids and heckling and disrespect from her husband. Having come from an emotionally abusive family, Sammi believed their behavior must be her fault. She must not deserve to be treated well.

As we worked together, Sammi began to learn to respect herself and believe that she was worthy of better treatment. As a result of this healthier attitude, she set limits with her family that required they treat her with respect. She stopped waffling between protest and capitulation and stuck by the consequences she had decided on if they reverted to their old behavior. One of those consequences was allowing herself to check into a nearby motel for several days and let her husband fend for himself and take care of the kids. When her family realized she would accept only the new, respectful behaviors, they began to change.

Although this wasn't easy for Sammi and required painful, yet freeing, self-examination and commitment to change, she created a safe house for herself in the very home that had once felt like an enemy camp. Like Sammi, we have the right to live (and work) in a safe environment; therefore, we need to teach people how to treat us by setting realistic and respectful limits and sticking by them.

❦

I deserve to live in a safe environment.

I have the courage to set limits and insist on respectful treatment.

I respect myself.

Befriending Fear

Worry often gives a small thing a big shadow.

—*Swedish proverb*

ONE OF THE HARDEST TASKS IN my life is to try and see fear as a positive growth-producing emotion rather than something to be avoided at all costs. Although probably none of us is ever going to be thrilled by the prospect of feeling afraid, we all need to demystify and declaw our fear by increasing our capacity to examine it. Unexplored fear has the tendency to clasp us powerfully in its grasp, thereby limiting our ability to live fully and happily. On the other hand, when we have the courage to look fear in the face, we often find a treasure house of self-awareness and unrealized potential.

Befriending fear by realizing that it has much to teach us is an important step on our path toward becoming our authentic, confident selves. Although it's not an easy task, viewing fear as a teacher is necessary in order for us to keep it from becoming a demanding and overbearing taskmaster. As I face my own fears, I use encouragement, comfort, and support from various sources; my desire here is to share some of those with you.

Risking Business

AS WOMEN LEAP DEEPER AND DEEPER into the often choppy waters of the business world, we face a new breed of fear. Will we succeed or fail? Can we swim with the sharks without becoming one? Do we have what it takes to capitalize on our knowledge, market our wares, and stay afloat in a sea of black, not red, ink?

Many of us are afraid to take the risks that seeing our dreams to fruition would require. One of the best ways to transform our fears is to discover how realistic they are. Some of our fears are based on fact and result from personal experiences; many others, however, are remnants of old inadequacies and beliefs from the past.

Do you have a dream? Is there a business you have secretly longed to participate in? Are you avoiding an occupational risk because of fear? If you answered yes to any of these questions it will be helpful for you to take some quiet time and do the following exercise. Divide a sheet of paper into three columns labeled: "My Dream" or "What I Would Like to Do"; "Fears Inhibiting Me"; and "How I Can Transform These Fears." Quickly jot down answers that come to you under the appropriate headings.

Give yourself the gift of facing your fears, gleaning self-awareness from them, and encouraging yourself to risk in spite of them. And remember to turn to friends for support and encouragement. Comforted by the response you receive as well as your own successes, you can more easily trust your abilities and maintain the courage to continue risking.

❦

I face my fears and learn from them.

I encourage myself to live my dreams.

I accept risk as a part of doing business.

Wisely Turning Tail

WE EACH HAVE INNER WISDOM THAT WE often disregard. We may instinctively know that a person or circumstance is not healthy for us, but still chide ourselves for foolishness or oversensitivity. In other words, we don't listen to the still, small voice inside us that *knows*. It's important that we begin paying attention to that voice, for it may be a bulletin from our wise self to turn tail and run.

Not heeding our interior oracle can cause us unnecessary pain. Anne, a young wife and mother, felt an innate dislike and distrust of another woman, Abbie, who was in her social crowd. But since everyone else in the group seemed to think Abbie was wonderful, Anne berated herself for feeling uncomfortable with her and made a special point of becoming her friend. As it turned out, Anne's instincts about Abbie were correct. Abbie, whose facade was unfailingly sweet, was a manipulative back-stabber and liar. Anne's failure to honor her intuition about Abbie and instead cultivate her "friendship" made it a double betrayal when Anne's husband walked out of her life and into Abbie's arms.

We constantly need to remind ourselves that we have an amazing wisdom—beyond our conscious perception—that often tries to warn us to stay away from certain people and experiences. Our job is to support ourselves by believing in and acting on these signals. Be alert to your inner cautions: sift through them, trusting that you know, deep down, what is good for you, and act on those that have external merit or persist internally. As Anne learned, it's sometimes very wise to honor our desire to turn tail and run.

I believe in my inner wisdom.

I honor my gut feelings by exploring them.

I support myself by acting on my intuition when appropriate.

Building on Small Successes

FOCUSING ON OUR SUCCESSES, NO MATTER how small, is an effective way to pare fear down to a manageable and realistic size. We all have everyday experiences that are successful and often have special and significant successes upon which we can also build. In order to have a happy and fulfilled life we need to focus on those "build-ups" rather than the "tear-downs." Yet it's so easy to habitually tear ourselves down by concentrating on our limitations rather than building on our successes.

For eighteen years Lynn was an active and involved at-home wife and mother. Her days were spent comforting and supporting her family, which included a hydrocephalic son who needed special attention. As the children grew, Lynn became increasingly restless and realized that she longed for a career as a computer troubleshooter.

Acknowledging her need to work outside the home in a challenging, male-dominated field created an eruption of fears in Lynn. She shared these fears with her women's group and, with their encouragement, began to work through her fears by taking one small step at a time and then building on that success. She experienced setbacks, of course, but congratulated herself on her success in weathering them and continued to persevere. In time, Lynn began believing and trusting in her abilities as a businesswoman.

Lynn is now the owner of a successful computer consulting business. Her road to success was paved with small steps, such as going to Adult Education classes, volunteering as a trainer for beginning computer students, working part-time, and doing small seminars for nominal fees. Her biggest accomplishments were surmounting her fear, overcoming barriers as they arose, and focusing on her modest successes one at a time.

Building a bridge of small successes can land us on the shore of our aspirations. What small, nonthreatening step can you take right now to help you befriend fear and build your own unique bridge?

I allow myself to take small steps toward my goals.

I accept and trust myself during both successful and difficult times.

Climbing the Peaks

I LIVE IN COLORADO, JUST AN HOUR FROM Rocky Mountain National Park. Being in the presence of those majestic, towering peaks, peaceful valleys, and pristine alpine lakes always puts me in a state of awed gratitude. Gratitude for both the beauty and the ruggedness—the grandeur of the massive mountains, the delicate, vulnerable beauty of the wild flowers, and the raw splendor of uninhabitable stretches of frozen tundra.

Our lives are similar to this impressive landscape. We all experience peaks of excitement and exhilaration, valleys of assimilation and rest, and chilling wastelands of depression and despair. Climbing out of the pits and up the peaks is one of our main occupations as human beings, and we need to trust that what is ultimately important is our overall progression. For often, to reach a peak, we need to take a circuitous route that can include doubling back and losing ground. At such times, the question to keep asking is: Am I generally moving forward and upward?

Quietly close your eyes and visualize where you are in your life today. Are you climbing a difficult slope toward the top of a peak, calmly camped in a verdant valley, or struggling in a seemingly bottomless pit? Allow yourself to be wherever you are. You are okay right here, right now. Very gently invite into your presence a supportive and encouraging Being who wants to assist you. If you are content where you are, then relax and enjoy the presence of your loving guide. If you would like to move out of the spot you're in, ask the Being if it will help you make the change. Agree to your Being's help and follow its guidance only if you feel totally nurtured and accepted by it.

Life is a series of ups and downs, and it is our responsibility to comfort and protect ourselves during this inevitable process. We have what it takes to become peak-conscious rather than pit-bound.

I honor and accept life with all its peaks and valleys.

I stand in awe of the variety in my life.

I love myself even if I am in the pits.

Jarring the Kaleidoscope

IF OUR LIVES ARE LIKE KALEIDOSCOPES, many of us spend a great deal of time and energy attempting to create the perfect picture—colors and shapes all exactly as we like them—and then want to set the resultant work of art in a place of honor, never to be moved again. This is it. Now we've finally got it right. Then, Crash! Bang! Life has a habit of bumping into our carefully constructed masterpiece, jarring it into a totally different image.

For years Laura had struggled with her belief that it was her job to "fix" any crisis or difficult circumstance that came up in her family and at work. With a great deal of psychological savvy, Laura courageously became aware of her need to control situations in a futile attempt to keep her kaleidoscope in the pattern she thought best.

Little by little Laura began to release her need for control, accept what she couldn't change, and increase her peace of mind. She was proud of her new kaleidoscope pattern and was enjoying it immensely when breast cancer jarred her life. After first raging and resisting the cancer, Laura came to believe that the stress induced by her old need to control and correct all situations had so depressed her immune system that cancer was the result.

But Laura is a fast learner, and she has now not only licked cancer but has truly given up another big C word: control. Laura now consistently accepts and trusts the varying kaleidoscope patterns in her life and, most important, realizes that she is not responsible for everyone else's patterns. Awareness was her first, and most important, step toward her healing.

Are there areas in your life where you need to let go of control and allow your kaleidoscope fragments the freedom to dance to their own tune?

I realize that it is not my job to be in control of everyone and everything.

I accept and enjoy my life in its beauty and imperfection.

I am healthy, happy, and hopeful.

Questing for the Holy Male

CINDERELLA RAN AWAY FROM THE PRINCE fearing that he would reject her if he knew who she really was, yet he searched for her and eventually took her away from a life of ashes and abuse to a happily-ever-after land. If we see the Cinderella myth as a metaphor for our inner process, we, too, often hightail it away from accepting our own masculine energy of dynamic creativity, leadership, and logical thinking, and then quest for an external male to carry these qualities for us.

This doesn't work. No one, not even the most wonderful man, can take the place of our own internal holy male. It is our scary, yet sacred, task to integrate both our feminine and masculine aspects into a balanced whole. If we are not aware of, or are frightened of, incorporating our masculine energy into our daily lives and instead look to a man for those qualities, we may have expectations that are unrealistically high or accept too little for fear of not being complete without him. In reality, the more we assimilate our male energy, the wiser we become in our selection of men as friends and mates.

Sit quietly and invite into your mind's eye a picture or symbol of your masculine self. If he is frightening, ask him why he feels the need to be threatening. If he is not a figure you can respect, ask him why he needs to appear weak. Allow yourself to get to know this part of yourself. What are his talents and fears, his dreams and aspirations? What qualities can he bring to your life? Befriend this important aspect of your being by asking him how he wants to be included in your daily life.

Incorporating our inner holy male and synthesizing our masculine and feminine selves brings us into a balance of doing and being—dynamic and magnetic energy—thereby creating a well-rounded whole.

I acknowledge and accept my masculine energy.

I explore any fears I have regarding my masculine aspects.

I am a well-rounded, multifaceted individual.

Living Our "Yes"

I SAW A NECKLACE, IN THE FORM OF A dog tag, with a single word, Yes!, engraved on it. What an enthusiastic affirmation of life! Sometimes fear, the great naysayer, gets in the way of our saying Yes to our dreams and talents and keeps us from reaching our highest potential.

Public speaking is one of my favorite ways to say Yes to living life to the fullest. I used to be absolutely terrified before giving a talk, but now I am usually only slightly nervous. Recently, however, I was catapulted back into almost paralyzing fear after seeing the publicity for an upcoming presentation. The little blurb on my talk outlined what people could hope to get from an evening with me, but I could not have delivered all they promised in a weekend workshop let alone the hour and a half I'd been allotted!

The Fear Serpent whispered convincingly, "They'll be disappointed. You'll be embarrassed." To still the voice, I did precisely the wrong thing—I ignored it. Because I was running away from my fear of failure, I resisted even preparing for the talk—a perfect way to set up the response I was dreading. Finally, at ten o'clock the night before my speech, I began to practice what I preach and explored my anxiety. Doing so helped me become aware of what I needed to do—take the fear out of my shadowy inner closet and share it with the audience. They, being fallible human beings also, could identify and empathize with me, and we ended up having a wonderful time learning from each other.

An excellent way to take fear out of overdrive is to strip it of secrecy: bring it out into the open. Crouching in darkness, fear hops in the driver's seat, but it begins to be transformed when brought into the light of awareness and acceptance.

In order to live our Yes!, we need to become aware of and accept our fear and then share it honestly where we will be gently accepted and supported.

❦

I am a strong and capable person even though I have fears.

I accept and support myself especially when I am feeling fearful.

Overcoming Goal Blindness

IT IS VERY EASY IN OUR RUSH, RUSH WORLD to be seduced into a state of goal blindness. By that I mean we become virtually blind to everything but the specific goal in front of us. When we're afflicted by such blindness, a gorgeous sunset, a friend's birthday, or even our own children's childhood, may come and go without our really paying attention. Reachable and realistic goals, interspersed with a few idealistic and hard-to-attain ones, are necessary and healthy; but being blinded by our goals—sacrificing spontaneity, fun, or family life for them—probably means we're being driven by some fear we need to uncover and heal.

Goal blindness leads to an imbalanced life. We are tyrannized by what "has to be done" and begin to dash through life as though it were a gourmet smorgasbord and we only had time for the bread. In order to lead a healthy life we need to balance inner and outer activities—stabilize the seesaw between doing and being, giving and receiving.

If you feel plagued by goal blindness, begin to free yourself by asking two questions: What fears are propelling me to work so compulsively? and, What is being sacrificed as I pursue this goal? As you answer, remember to do so in a loving and nonjudgmental way. You are doing the best you can, and are now in the process of making some new choices. That's a decision that deserves praise, not punishment. Next ask yourself this question: What small step am I willing to take right now to bring my life into better balance?

Goal blindness leads to rushing, and rushing is dehumanizing and injurious to all living beings, including ourselves. Although it's hard to break the habit of rushing blindly toward our goals, we can do it. With awareness, willingness, and commitment, we can learn to sample in a more leisurely fashion all the delicacies life has to offer.

❦

I give myself permission to bite off only as much as I can comfortably digest.

I take one small step at a time toward rebalancing my life.

Standing by Our Core

THE WORD "COURAGE" COMES FROM A combination of *cor*, which in Latin means "heart," and *corage*, which is French for "the capacity to stand by our core." Standing by our core by having the courage to honor ourselves and value our needs is often difficult if we've been taught to put others first and ourselves second, if at all. It takes a great deal of heart to counter old beliefs about the appropriateness of standing up for ourselves.

Often we feel unsure about living in integrity with our core because we fear moving into a "me, me, me" mode of selfish behavior. The opposite is actually true. The more we honor ourselves by standing by our core beliefs and feelings, the more loving toward others we become.

When Meryl, a talented actress, left her husband, their friends were shocked because they had seemed like an ideal couple. In reality Meryl's husband was abusive, jealous, and demeaning in private. For years Meryl's best acting role was the one she played off stage—the happy and contented wife. Meryl feared she must be doing something wrong to elicit such behavior from her husband and she tried to change, but nothing worked.

Finally, after being painfully injured during one of her husband's outbursts, Meryl began believing that she didn't deserve such treatment. With the support of a therapist, she mustered the courage to face her fears and really value herself. In the process, she found that her capacity to love her daughter and others began to expand. The energy she had used protecting her family's secret by pretending all was well was now free to flow unchecked—even toward her former husband.

Having the heart to stand by our core requires that we pare away the layers of "he wants," "they expect," and "I should" in order to find the "I am," "I need," and "I can." By sensitively healing the fears causing us to betray our core, we can become accepting and supportive lovers to ourselves and others.

❦

I have the right to honor who I am, what I need, and what I can do.

I have the heart to love and support myself.

Remodeling the Rescuer

ALTHOUGH WOMEN ARE LEARNING TO stop accepting responsibility for other people's feelings, we still seem prone to embrace blame readily. In fact we often act like blame magnets, collecting bits and pieces of negative mental pain and resentment, and believe we are charged with the rescue of the senders. This is an extremely uncomfortable way to live. In order to truly live in comfort with ourselves, we need to make a concerted effort to renovate our internal rescuer by permitting other people to rescue themselves.

Georgia remodeled her rescuer in one of the most difficult "fix it" relationships to give up—that of mother and adult child. Georgia's daughter Carrie, a sensitive and artistic young woman, had a series of semi-nervous breakdowns. The entire family went to counseling, then Georgia and her husband financed Carrie's return to college. When Carrie flunked out of school, her parents hired her to work in their business, but she took advantage of the situation by consistently arriving late, if at all, and not doing the work assigned.

Georgia agonized over Carrie's plight ("What have I done to cause my daughter's weakness?") and made exceptions that she wouldn't have made for a regular employee. The situation got worse and worse. Now, although it is heartbreaking for her, Georgia is little by little allowing Carrie to deal with the consequences of her actions. In order to have the courage not to race to the rescue, but to let Carrie take responsibility for her own actions, Georgia constantly reminds herself that she did the best she knew how in parenting her child and that Carrie is now an adult in charge of her own life.

Our need to rescue comes from both the desire to alleviate others' pain and a sense of blame or responsibility. Relieving pain, when it is possible, is good, but taking blame or responsibility is often a destructive pattern of behavior we learned early in our lives. We can transform that legacy by lovingly allowing others to rescue themselves in all appropriate times and ways.

❦

I assume total responsibility for my own actions.

I allow others to take responsibility for their own lives.

Leaving the Mists of "Someday I'll"

WE ARE SURROUNDED BY INNUMERABLE opportunities. Possibilities for personal expansion, excitement, and happiness abound. Do we take advantage of them or do we crouch fearfully in the shadows saying, "Someday I'll learn to speak up for myself, clear up this relationship, write my book," etcetera?

Someday I'll does not honor the present, create a positive future or support our self-esteem. Hiding in the mists of *Someday I'll* may appear safe but usually leaves us filled with regret for things left undone and unsaid.

But what if we're frightened about doing or being something new and have relegated the desired change to "maybe tomorrow"? We need to transform our fear by having the courage to look at it and heal it. We can start by asking ourselves what is keeping us stuck.

Mary, a former teacher, had been struggling with what career path to follow as she entered her fifties. For two years she investigated different options but nothing held her attention for very long. Mary began to explore her fears in depth and discovered that she had been a very demanding taskmaster with herself in all areas of her life, including her teaching—everything had to be perfect or it was unacceptable. She came to understand that she was frightened to start a new vocation for fear she would once more beat herself up with unrealistic requirements.

Mary's commitment to let go of perfectionism assisted her in her decision to enter the seminary. At the age of fifty-two, she's left the mists of *Someday I'll*, in part by assuring herself that she will pursue the ministry only "as long as it continues to feel right!" By adopting a tolerant and flexible attitude such as this, Mary is free to follow her calling.

If you have a dream languishing in the mists of *Someday I'll*, gently encourage yourself to examine any fears that may be keeping you from realizing your dream right now. In the warmth of loving self-support, our fears can dissipate and we are empowered to confidently follow our heart's lead.

I make decisions easily.
I allow myself to follow my heart's lead.
I do it now.

Transforming Inner Tyrants

WE ALL HAVE AN INNER CAST OF characters that I call sub-personalities. Often these internal family members remain strangers to us, neither accepted nor synthesized into our lives. Sub-personalities are formed or *de-formed* around our beliefs and assumptions and, if unrecognized, can cause us to act and feel in ways that are detrimental to our well-being.

We can integrate the estranged parts of ourselves by becoming aware of their fears, wants, and needs. Each of our sub-personalities has, at its core, a positive quality. Acceptance allows that quality to manifest itself in our lives.

Sit quietly with your eyes closed and gently invite your inner cast members to appear, as though on a stage. They may emerge as people, symbols, animals, or just as a sense or feeling. Without judgment observe them from a distance. What do they look like? How do they feel? Are they comfortable or uncomfortable, happy or sad, calm or angry? And very important, how do you feel toward them?

Choose the sub-personality about whom you feel the most accepting and begin to get acquainted with it. For a few moments, just be together, sensing how you feel about each other. Is there trust and respect, love and acceptance? What quality does this inner family member have that you would like expressed more in your life? Ask it what it wants and needs from you. Are you willing to give that?

Now do the same exercise with the sub-personality who most disturbs you. Remember that *each* aspect of ourselves, no matter how vile it may appear or act, has at its center a positive quality. When liberated from the dark cellar of our subconscious into the light of our acceptance, it can become a creative spiritual force within us.

Tenderly befriending and supporting all our cast members allows them to transform from inner tyrants into trusted friends.

All parts of me are good at their center.

I heal and transform my wounded inner selves by loving and accepting them.

Disappearing into Availability

OUT OF A DESIRE TO DO THE RIGHT THING or a fear of rejection, we can make ourselves so available to those we love that we become invisible to them. We disappear as a person and become merely an anonymous constant to be taken for granted. Amy Tan, author of *The Joy Luck Club*, wrote, "My Amah loved me so much that I no longer saw her except as a convenience there to serve me."

If we feel lost in a labyrinth of other people's demands and desires, we need to look beneath our facade of helpfulness and unearth any unhealthy fears or beliefs we have that are allowing us to be taken for granted.

To help yourself discover areas where you disappear into availability, write a list of circumstances in which you feel used or taken for granted. For each separate entry ask yourself why you continue to act in a way that results in your feeling invisible and undervalued.

If your answer begins something like, "I'm afraid that...," question your fear: Is it realistic? Is this an old fear from childhood that has no validity in your current life? Who, in your inner cast of characters, is experiencing the fear?

What do they need from you to help alleviate their fear? If your fear is realistic, what is the worst thing that could happen if you changed your behavior? Do you have the maturity and wisdom to support yourself emotionally if the worst scenario was realized? Although it's not easy to change patterns of over-accommodating behavior, we can do so by assuring ourselves that we have the right and the need to be available to ourselves as well, which, in turn, will make us less resentful of and more loving toward others. Healthy availability enhances relationships, but self-denial and overindulgence destroys them. It's necessary for our well-being—and the good of humanity—that we are available to others, but it is essential that we honor and support ourselves in the process.

I am available to others in a way that enhances their life and mine.

I deserve to be visible and valued.

Becoming the Parent
We Deserve

How badly the child needs a mediator,
someone who can understand both
worlds—heart and intellect—and help
bring them a little closer together.

—Irene Claremont de Castillejo

SO MANY OF US HAVE NEGATIVE parental voices inside of us that shame and discourage us. It's hard to have self-confidence and peace of mind when we are consistently castigating ourselves. But we can change those critical voices to supportive and comforting ones by becoming the parent we deserve to have.

I recently heard someone say, "If you've had parents, you need therapy." Right. None of us had perfect parents nor are *we* perfect parents, but no matter how abusive our home life may have been, or how deep our scars, we have the ability to become a nurturing parent to ourselves now. Even if our childhoods were idyllic, there are still ways in which we can benefit from becoming more supportive of ourselves today.

Quieting the Critic

DO YOU CARRY ON AN OMNIPRESENT monologue with yourself that is critical? So many of us do. We relive how we flubbed up, beating ourselves into the ground with a litany of real and imagined sins and shortcomings.

Who do you suppose is talking when we discredit and discourage ourselves? Often it is our mother's or father's voice, as we remember it, from a nonsupportive childhood. A good example is Jody, whose stepfather sexually molested her for years. When she finally told her mother, her mother said she should be ashamed of herself for lying and that if such a thing were to happen, Jody would probably have asked for it. Not surprisingly, Jody's self-critical voice condemned her with constant censure as an adult. When I asked her to see who was talking as she attacked herself, a picture of her mother appeared in her mind.

The following meditation helped Jody quiet her inner critic. For a few moments, with your eyes closed, allow yourself to listen carefully to your critical inner voice. Does it sound like anyone you know? Very gently allow a picture of the speaker to come into your mind's eye. It may appear as someone familiar or it may be a stranger, an animal, or a symbol. Ask the speaker why she is being so critical. Ask what it would take for her to speak to you more gently.

If she is not willing to work with you on becoming more encouraging and supportive, enclose her in a barrier that makes it impossible for her to reach you. (Jody put her uncooperative mother in a strong bubble of light where she could see her but not hear her.) Now invite into your mental picture a comforting parent who speaks lovingly—an internal parent with whom you feel safe. Bask in her healing presence.

In order to quiet our inner critic we need to personify it, protect ourselves from it, and then replace it. No matter who the voice belonged to in the past, it is ours now and we can change it.

❦

I deserve to be spoken to in encouraging ways.

*I have the power to change my critical
inner voice to a loving and supportive one.*

Living in
Mr. Rogers' Neighborhood

AS WE BECOME THE PARENT WE DESERVE, it's very important that we choose to live in the right neighborhood. By that I mean we choose to associate with people who help us support and feel good about ourselves.

The children's TV program "Mr. Rogers' Neighborhood" is great for the child in all of us. At the end of the show the gentle and caring Mr. Rogers looks directly at us and says, "You've made this day a very special day for me. How? Just by being *you!* You're the kind of person it's easy to like."

Sometimes our neighbors—family, co-workers, friends—aren't so encouraging as Mr. Rogers. For years Rosemary had done everything she could to create a loving relationship with her sister. But still her sister seemed to thrive on putting Rosemary down.

As Rosemary unhappily learned, our family members are sometimes not our best neighbors. But even Christ did not expect us to love all people in a personal way. He encouraged us to love with agape—impersonal, benevolent love—wishing others well and having concern for them although not necessarily feeling lovey-dovey.

We need to protect ourselves from others' toxicity. Who of us would hug a porcupine in full bristle or stroke a skunk with its tail raised? Yet because of guilt and "shoulds" we sometimes allow ourselves to be pricked and poisoned by relatives or so-called friends.

If we are to create a Mr. Rogers' neighborhood for ourselves, we need to give ourselves permission to move out of the range of emotionally destructive behavior, even when it's that of a relative. From a safe distance, we can begin to send them impersonal love darts. If you feel too vulnerable or angry to send love, it may help to visualize yourself in the protective arms of a teacher or guide. From the shelter of that embrace, you can feel safe to open your heart and send compassion to the hurtful person.

❧

I deserve to be treated well.

I have the right not to relate to people who treat me poorly.

I create a loving and supportive neighborhood for myself.

Bumping Negativity
Off the Agenda

THERE IS A PHRASE IN THE COMPUTER profession that says, "garbage in, garbage out." It means that if a program is set up poorly and gives erroneous messages to the computer, it will yield only garbled output. Our minds work on much the same principle. If we put garbage such as negativity into our minds, our lives will reflect it by being more difficult and less joyful than we wish they were.

If, out of habit, we have been placing negative thinking at the top of our life's agenda, we need to bump it to the very bottom—with the goal of eliminating it altogether. As we replace negativity with upbeat and optimistic thinking, we create an environment where the seeds of creativity, humor, and love can take root.

Math is the only arena where a negative times a negative equals a positive. In the real life of emotions and beliefs, compounded negatives equal only more negatives. So when we allow our minds to dwell on pessimistic feelings and thoughts we develop a mental magnet that draws more negativity to us.

We can change that by a simple mental exercise. On days when you are feeling low, it's important to support yourself by first becoming aware of your negative thoughts, then by consciously placing each one—one at a time—on the bottom of your mental agenda. Finally, put a comforting, affirming thought at the top of your agenda. Although this exercise may seem phony at first, persevere and you will begin to create a new habit of "positive in, positive out."

I am committed to being a positive thinker.

I support myself by converting negative thoughts into positive ones.

I deserve to have a positive and fulfilling life.

Blessings of
Our Natural Child

MOST OF US ARE AWARE OF OUR
wounded inner child and experience her
regularly. But inside of us is also a natural, play-
ful child. She may be buried deeply under layers of distrust and injury, but she is there and we
can recover her. As we become a loving parent
to ourselves, she will begin to emerge and we'll
discover a little person who is curious rather
than fearful, spontaneous rather than rigid,
helpful instead of resistant, creative instead of
bored, and open rather than wary.

If the spontaneous, carefree part of ourselves
has gone into hiding, it's probably because we
have been overly harsh with ourselves and unin-
tentionally created an emotional climate in
which our natural child could not thrive. The
best way to encourage her to appear is to make
it safe for her to do so. By treating ourselves
gently, we issue an invitation to the little girl
that says, "It's safe to be here, Honey! You're
welcome to come out and play. I promise you'll
be appreciated, valued, and protected."

On the afternoon before she was to have a

mastectomy, Charlene, whose wounded inner child was terrified about the upcoming surgery, visualized her natural little girl and asked her what she'd like to do before going into the hospital. Unhesitatingly she answered, "Take Peaches for a walk and go barefoot in the creek!" To the casual observer it looked as though a gray-haired lady and her dog were romping in the creek; to Charlene it was a healing and soothing outing with two little kids—one fearful, the other trusting and adventurous.

Do yourself the service of recovering your natural inner child. She will bless your life with joy, laughter, and spontaneity.

❧

I am a gentle and loving parent to myself.
I invite my natural inner child into my everyday life.
I protect myself and my inner children.

Accentuating the Functional

IT IS WONDERFUL THAT WE NO LONGER deny the dysfunction of our families of origin or even the families we created; but there is a danger now that we may dwell on the dysfunction and deny any nurturing we received. Almost all of us have moments in our past when we felt loved and supported. Remembering those good times underscores and bolsters our belief in our own loveability.

Allowing ourselves to recall pleasant memories facilitates our healing and fosters forgiveness of both our parents and ourselves as parents. None of us had—or were—perfect parents, but there are probably at least slivers of healthy recollections that we can give thanks for.

If we're suffering stabs of guilt over how we have been parenting our children, it's especially important that we accentuate our functional behavior in order to build on it. If we persist in emphasizing our dysfunctional actions, we will only discourage ourselves and make healthy change more difficult.

In a quiet alone time, or with a trusted friend, make a list of any times you remember being happy or contented as a child. Replay those minutes or hours. Savor them. Relive the feelings and give thanks for the experiences. Then make a separate list of times you have felt pleased with and proud of your own parenting skills. Share those memories with your mate, children, or a friend. Give yourself credit for a job well done.

Accentuating the functional encourages us to trust ourselves. It gives us a surplus of strength we can draw on for support when we need to look at dysfunction in our life in order to heal it and move on.

I am thankful for my past—both the challenging and the rewarding parts of it.

I accentuate the positive in my background without denying the painful.

I am a caring parent to myself and my children.

Reframing Family Pictures

IN LEARNING TO LOVINGLY RE-PARENT ourselves, it's a good idea to look at the family album we carry inside our heads. Some of the snapshots will evoke happy memories and warm fuzzy feelings while others may seem more like potshots aimed hurtfully at us. A great many of our internal images were developed when we were young and had a child's less-than-powerful perspective. As adults, we now have the authority to reframe painful memories much the same way we might change the frames of pictures displayed on the piano.

Give yourself some time to mentally browse through the photos you've accumulated from your past. Choose one that seems to call attention to itself. Very gently become the child you see there. Even more gently ask her what she wants and needs from you. Are you willing to fulfill her wish? If you feel loving and protective of her, allow your adult self to comfort her in the ways she requests. If you don't feel good toward her, bring into your mind's eye a protector who does feel loving toward her. Allow this individual to care for your child.

With the help of either your adult self or the

person you call in to assist, redevelop the uncomfortable snapshot into a picture in which your little girl is safe and happy. Sense her feelings as she experiences life from this different viewpoint. Absorb and claim those feelings as rightfully yours. Now put your new memory picture in a beautiful, valuable frame and display it in a prominent place.

If you find yourself reverting to the distressing feelings of the original picture, move your thoughts to the new one and remind yourself that as an empowered adult, you can reframe your child's painful perspective.

I can view old experiences in the new light of my adult empowerment.

I take care of my inner child by honoring her wants and needs.

Completing
Unfinished Business

LIKE A NAGGING ACHE OR PAIN, unfinished business is enervating and discouraging. It can include things we regret having said, kindnesses left undone, muddied misunderstandings, or times we wished we had stood up for ourselves. In the bereavement groups I conducted for many years, unfinished business was one of the most difficult aspects of the grief that people experienced; they regretted that death had robbed them of the chance to do things differently with a person they loved.

Finishing business that's been left dangling, repairing ruptured relationships, and taking the time to say things we feel but rarely express are healthy ways of emotionally supporting ourselves. Clearing up unfinished business alleviates emotional pain, builds self-esteem, and adds to our peace of mind by bringing a sense of completeness to our lives.

I'd like to share with you my three R's for completing business. First *redo*. If there is something we regret doing and it is possible to redo it through taking a new, different action, we can do so. Second, we need to make *reparation*; we can have the courage to accept responsibility for anything we did that was hurtful or harmful to others and sincerely apologize. Third, it is important that we know when to *release* our feelings about any injury we have caused or sustained. Redo, make reparation, and then release any residual guilt or shame.

When you have finished your business to the best of your ability, comfort yourself by releasing what can't be changed and congratulate yourself on completing what can be healed.

I am committed to completing unfinished business.

I have the courage to apologize for past errors.

I release what can't be changed.

Seeing Our Parents Small

ALTHOUGH IT'S SOMETIMES HARD FOR us to believe, our parents were once children too! Many of them lived through the upheaval of world war and the uncertainty of the Great Depression. Almost none of them were encouraged to experience or express what they felt. In their day you did not "air your dirty laundry in public" or "wear your heart on your sleeve." Instead you "pulled yourself up by your bootstraps" and "kept a stiff upper lip." Is it any wonder that we, in turn, sometimes felt repressed as children?

A large part of becoming the parents we deserve is to understand, honor, and forgive the parents we had. This meditation can help. Settle yourself comfortably in a quiet place and pay attention to your breathing. Without effort observe yourself inhaling and exhaling. Deepen your breath and, as you inhale, draw in a sense of safety from the universe. As you exhale, let go of any resistance or fear you may be experiencing. Very gently invite into your awareness a picture, or a sense, of your mother as a little girl. How do you feel toward her? If it feels right to you, move toward getting to know her—talk to her, be with her. As you begin to feel complete with this meeting, in your mind's eye shrink your little-girl mother until she is very tiny and, when it feels right to you, tuck her into your heart. Repeat the process with your father.

Seeing our parents small allows us to form a different picture of them. If they have intimidated, abandoned, or disappointed us, seeing them small helps us understand some of their pain and vulnerability. From that empowered position we can learn to tuck them into our hearts and love them more readily. Accepting our parents' inner little child helps us love and accept our own.

I want to understand and forgive my parents.

I love and accept my vulnerable inner child and my parents' as well.

I tuck my parents into my heart.

Stopping the Sacrifice Cycle

WOMEN OFTEN CONFUSE SACRIFICE WITH service. Sometimes we have the underlying belief that not only should we give away our hopes, dreams, time, and energy in the service of others, but we should also feel good about doing so. We have the idea that we're only okay if we willingly sacrifice ourselves on the altar of family, job, and charitable causes.

Judy became aware that she had accepted a belief passed from generation to generation by the women in her family, namely that *we give up what we want, actually who we are, when we marry.* Judy's mother gave up a promising singing career when she married, and, unconsciously following the pattern set by her, Judy—who loved to travel—married a man who disapproved of traveling and allowed her to go out of town only occasionally to see her parents. The one time she defied him by driving to the next state to visit a friend, he didn't speak to her for three days.

In every way she knew how Judy tried to salvage her marriage, but when it became clear that in order to do so she would need to continue to sacrifice not only her desire to travel but her intelligence, authority, and wisdom, she divorced her husband. And although she would have liked to remarry, she shied away from becoming involved with anyone for several years while she worked on freeing herself from the family beliefs she'd been perpetuating. Judy consciously stopped the sacrifice cycle and is now in a committed relationship with a wonderful man who honors and admires her individuality.

We can break the sacrifice cycle when we stop confusing sacrifice with service and grow to trust that we deserve to create relationships that support both our selves and our dreams.

I have a right to be who I am and to pursue my hopes and dreams.

I maintain a sense of myself, both alone and in relationships.

I enjoy being of service to myself and others.

Creating a New Family Myth

ALL FAMILIES HAVE TRADITIONAL STORIES about "how we do it in this family." Some of the myths are positive and provide the backbone of our strengths; others, however, need editing and overhauling because they are outmoded and limiting to us. As we master the art of re-parenting ourselves we'll probably want to rewrite at least a few of our family myths.

Megan's IQ ranks in the low genius category, but one of her family's myths cheated her out of higher education when she was young. Her family believed that boys were smart and therefore had the right to go to college, while girls were supposed to learn the skills that would make them good homemakers. Until the girls married, it was their job to work and contribute to their brothers' education. Being a dutiful daughter, Megan first helped support her brother through law school; then she married and worked while her husband got his engineering degree.

Take a few moments to review some of your family myths. Are they fact or fable? Do they enhance your life or diminish it? Does your self-esteem soar or suffer in the light of these traditions? Are these legacies that you want to pass on to your children?

We have different awarenesses and insights than our families of origin did. We are the authors of our lives and have the power not only to change what no longer works for us but to create supportive and encouraging family myths—ones that liberate rather than limit us. Megan, for example, is creating a new story for herself, her children, and grandchildren. At age seventy-eight she is completing her college degree. You can rewrite your story, too.

❧

I rewrite my story in a way that supports me.

I create family myths for myself and my children that are empowering and energizing.

Being Our Own Midwife

SINCE LIFE IS A CONTINUAL PROGRESSION of birth and rebirth, becoming the parent we deserve includes accepting the role of midwife to ourselves as we labor to live authentically. As adults dedicated to being ourselves in order to truly love and be loved by others, we need to commit ourselves to the often painful process of being reborn into new beliefs and behaviors.

One of the scariest aspects of letting go of the old and welcoming the new is fear of change. Stepping out into unknown emotional territory is only possible when we trust that ultimately we will be safe doing so. Toward that end, being our own midwife means that we gently protect our vulnerable infant self, which fears abandonment and betrayal, as we courageously undergo the process of giving birth to our genuine selves.

In a quiet, protected time and space, close your eyes and allow yourself to deeply relax by using whatever technique works best for you. Sink luxuriously into the warm darkness of your breath and become conscious of the beating of your heart. Concentrate on the rhythm of your heartbeat and become part of it. Tenderly imagine yourself in the womb of an all-loving mother who is awaiting your arrival with great anticipation.

Effortlessly begin your trip through the birth canal, and, as you slip free of your mother's body, feel yourself caught in the embrace of a strong and accepting midwife. Experience the joy of being handed to a devoted mother who, with great pride, shows you to the welcoming and supportive family which has been excitedly waiting for you. Soak up the comfort of being totally loved and accepted.

I am a loving midwife to myself as I incorporate new beliefs and behaviors into my life.

I lovingly accept myself.

Reclaiming Childhood Dreams

WERE YOU EVER TOLD TO STOP BEING silly when you fantasized and imagined as a child? Were your dreams endorsed and encouraged or were they scoffed at by the big people you looked up to? What about now? Are the people in your life, including yourself, supportive of your aspirations? Many of the hopes, desires, and dreams we had as children were indicators of the special gifts we brought into this life. If we have lost track of our dreams, we can reconnect with them now by encouraging ourselves to look back and explore them.

We can reconnect with our dreams and lovingly support ourselves in pursuing them by asking questions such as: What make-believe did I revel in when I was little? Where did I go in my fantasy world? What did I want to be when I grew up? Where was my safe and secret place? And then, very importantly, ask: How can I translate my childhood dreams into adult realities?

As a little kid I loved to dress up and perform "plays" I had written. In my adult life I've done quite a bit of community theater, but at this stage in my life I'm concentrating on writing and am not willing to devote the time that acting requires, so I do little plays for myself—especially while driving. I include other motorists in my cast and practice dialects on them. When watching TV, I often verbally interact with the characters. In other words, I let myself *play* like I used to when I was little. If my critical inner voice begins to interfere, I transform it into a comforting parental voice that assures me I'm not crazy, just creative.

Our childhood dreams and fantasies are gold mines of possibility. Denying dreams dulls us, but accepting them can energize and motivate us to expand into areas that our hearts have yearned for throughout a lifetime. Take the opportunity now to reclaim your unique dreams.

❦

I honor and listen to my dreams—current and past.

I give myself permission to play.

I have the right to dream and explore possibilities.

Excusing the Jury

MANY OF US ARE LIVING UNDER THE tyranny of an internal jury that seems to delight in pronouncing us guilty for the slightest violation of the rules. If we regularly subject ourselves to self-inflicted judgments, we tend to live in a constant state of stress and distress. Instead of experiencing antagonistic counsel beating us at (and with) the bar, we can bring into our lives supportive and comforting counselors.

It is up to us to transform our internal jury by realizing, at a deep level, that we have a right to be who and what we are. We can empower ourselves by changing the jury to a loving and supportive group of ethical advisors. This type of change isn't easy and it takes plenty of desire and discipline, but we do have the power to alter our internal cast of characters from vengeful judges to benevolent supporters.

Take a few minutes to remember a time when your inner jury was berating you. Without trying to change them, listen to those inner voices. Observe your feelings as you are subjected to the harangue. Take a step back and begin to visualize who is speaking to you. Give faces to the jury members, picturing them in as much detail as you can.

Now ask for assistance from a wise and loving counselor who can help you excuse this unruly jury and install in its place a loyal fan club. If the counselor who appears is not totally supportive and 100 percent in favor of the transformation, this is not the right person. Invite him or her to leave, and ask for your real counselor to come into your mind's eye. With his or her help, visualize each jury member being replaced by a benevolent and fair booster. When the image of your fan club is complete, take a few moments to luxuriate in their acceptance and encouragement.

I have the right to be me.

I invite into my internal and external lives supportive and encouraging people.

Embracing
No-Fault Living

*I always see the good that is in people
and leave the bad to Him who made
mankind and knows how to round off
the corners.*

—Goethe's mother

So MANY RELATIONSHIPS FLOUNDER on the rocks of disapproval and blame. In order to enjoy comfortable, companionable, and mutually supportive relationships, we need to embrace the art of no-fault living. This doesn't mean that we become a patsy and allow others to walk all over us, but it does mean that we learn to curb our criticism of others and insist they do the same toward us.

No-fault living includes accepting and supporting ourselves, our friends, and our loved ones. No-fault living builds up confidence; it means never putting down or making fun of ourselves or others. When there are uncomfortable issues to confront, we discuss them in a way that leads to understanding and solutions but doesn't cast blame.

Everyone is imperfect, and having that fact pointed out to us in a critical fashion (and is there really any other way to do it?) decreases our chances of expanding and enhancing our capabilities. In the face of censure, we become fearful of doing or saying anything and learn to walk on eggshells. Criticism dams the flow of good feelings, whereas encouragement and support strengthen our ability to become the best person we are capable of being.

Irrigating Arid Situations

MANY OF US WHO ARE CONCERNED about the environment are landscaping our yards with plants and shrubs that are drought resistant and can thrive with very little care and maintenance, creating what is called a xeriscape. This is a responsible thing to do so far as our yards are concerned, but it's not so good for our personal lives. How many of us live arid emotional lives, barely able to maintain our root system let alone bloom beautifully, on the amount of emotional sustenance we receive?

In order to emotionally support ourselves, we need to become gently honest with ourselves about whether or not our lives and relationships are supporting us—giving us enough love and attention to thrive—or whether we're dying of thirst. And we also need to examine whether we are providing enough of the emotional essentials for those we love.

If we have settled for a situation that is barren, we need to find ways to bring it back to life or, if that isn't possible, to create other oases for ourselves—people who appreciate us, activities that fulfill us, hobbies that give us a sense of worth and pleasure.

We can learn to water our own landscape and create a flourishing garden out of our life. Quietly close your eyes and visualize yourself in a verdant garden. Browse leisurely through the beauty of this special place where you sense you truly belong. Feel yourself uplifted by the sights and smells of this magical oasis. Find a welcoming spot and make yourself comfortable. Now imagine what flower you might be if you were a resident of this garden. What do you need to keep you healthy and blooming? In what small way can you begin to bring this nourishment into your daily life?

If we're struggling to survive in a xeriscape, we can change that by paying better attention to our wants and needs, and finding and creating springs where we can quench our thirst. From our overflow, we will generously spill out love to others.

From a sense of overflow, I give to myself and others.

I deserve to be cherished and appreciated.

Owning Our
Own Projections

ONE OF THE BEST WAYS TO ENSURE
fulfilling relationships is to be confident of who
we are and have an honest and supportive relationship with ourselves. Why is this so important? Because, to the extent that we don't know
ourselves or are blind to our vulnerabilities and
prejudices, we will unknowingly project those
shortcomings onto our relationships with others.

For instance, if we berate and judge ourselves
when we make a mistake, we're likely to think
that other people are also judging us when, in
fact, they may be completely unaware of the
mistake.

We need to become aware when we say
things such as "He won't let me" or "They don't
listen" if we are actually projecting an internal
feeling that "I don't trust myself to do that" or "I
don't listen to myself because I fear I don't have
anything of value to contribute." If we are projecting, it is our internal scripts, and the feelings
creating those scripts, that need editing and re-
vision.

It is impossible to ask "them" to treat us in ways we do not yet treat ourselves. Therefore, we need to consciously realize when we are projecting our unfinished business onto others so that we can reclaim those projections and heal the erroneous self-concepts that created them.

We are the authors of our lives, and we can write new, healthy scripts that cast us as lovable and deserving women. As a result, we're more likely to be appreciated by those around us and our relationships consequently will be enhanced.

❧

I am willing to acknowledge my own projections.

I have the courage to heal emotional wounds that keep me from having good relationships.

I love and support myself.

Throwing Out the Gauntlet

THROWING DOWN THE GAUNTLET IS AN invitation to a duel; it's issuing a challenge—in effect, sticking our chins out and saying, "I dare you!" While this kind of attitude may be apropos for sports or other contests, it is not conducive to developing harmonious personal relationships. Mutually supportive partners do not issue challenges through the gauntlets of blame or competition—both loud calls to dueling. Instead, they are committed to eliminating blame and playing fair. Cooperation, not challenge, leads to satisfying relationships.

If we find ourselves having an aggressive attitude in a relationship, we need to throw the gauntlet *out* into the trash, not *down* in front of the other person. When we're dedicated to learning to live supportively, we choose to communicate in ways that allow us to complement rather than compete with each other, ways that foster harmony rather than dissent.

Sit quietly, close your eyes, and allow to effortlessly arise in your mind a relationship in which you are locking horns with someone, a situation that is a challenge and frustration to you. View this predicament nonjudgmentally.

What gauntlet have you thrown down? What blame are you casting? What challenge have you been unwilling to accept?

In your mind's eye, gently step back from the scene and picture it as though from your higher self. Ponder how you might eliminate blame and bridge the troublesome impasse by approaching it with a goal toward understanding and cooperation rather than convincing and winning.

Since it's difficult to remain open and vulnerable when faced with an adversary, intimacy is usually the casualty of a thrown-down gauntlet The old proverb about catching more bees with honey is true: with supportive attitudes and a desire to understand, we can "catch" more sweetness in our lives.

***

I find myself and others blameless.

I communicate nonjudgmentally with the goal of understanding.

Figuring Out Who's Fighting

So many of our feelings stem from old fears we keep buried in the trunk of our past. When these feelings surface, we may act irrationally, baffling and scaring those—including ourselves—who experience the brunt of our emotions. Often, out of frustration and bewilderment, fights erupt. In order to sort things out, we need to figure out who's fighting.

Lana and her fiancé, Mitchell, were having a terrible argument. In the face of her seemingly irrational fear of getting married, he had withdrawn into an icy silence. As a result, she felt abandoned and screamed at him that she was canceling the wedding. In response he disgustedly left the house. Sobbing, she called me. After listening to her story, I asked her who was feeling abandoned. In a moment, she thoughtfully said, "Oh! I think it's me at about three years old."

As a three-year-old, Lana had good reason to fear abandonment; now her adult self was acting out that old fear in response to the marriage commitment she was about to make. She told Mitchell who it was in her inner cast of characters that was fearful, and he was able to realize that he wasn't intimidated by Lana's inner three-year-old. But, *his* insecure little boy had been terrified by what he saw as a raging adult rejecting him.

The insights Mitchell and Lana gleaned from their premarital confrontation led them to make a commitment to help each other figure out "who's fighting" when seemingly groundless feelings arise in the future. With a renewed appreciation for each other's sensitivity and vulnerability, and an awareness that they could comfort and support their own and each other's scared inner child, they were married as scheduled.

If baffling feelings grab you by the guts and fights threaten to erupt as a result, ask yourself who is in the grip of the emotion. You'll probably come face-to-face with an old fear. The bearer of that fear needs and deserves your acceptance and reassurance.

I support myself emotionally by figuring out who, inside, is the bearer of scary feelings.

I comfort and support my needy inner child.

Living Gently
with Ourselves and Others

LONG BEFORE GEORGE BUSH BEGAN talking about a kinder, gentler nation, my personal stationery carried the reflection, *Live gently with yourself and others*. People regularly respond to that thought by saying something like, "I wish I *could* live more gently!"

One way for us to learn the art of gentle living is to keep the word, *gentle* or *gently*, in our awareness. Gentle, along with its synonyms *kind, considerate, patient*, and *tender*, is easily lost in the hubbub of our demanding days. In the course of our normal schedules, the concept of gentleness rarely occurs to us.

As I was retraining myself to live gently with myself rather than harshly, I put little cards reading "Gently" in my wallet, on the fridge, on my desk, and in my journal. Each time I saw the word I was reminded that there was a different— a supportive and comforting—way for me to treat myself and others. Now, when I tune into negative self-talk or judgmental feelings toward myself or someone else, I eventually remember to ask, "Is this gentle?" Often, just that little nudge helps me move from a prickly to a soft place within myself.

Choose an evening when you can have some meditative time for yourself and allow your mind to roam back over the day or week. Were there times when you would like to have acted more gently or adopted a more gentle attitude? If so, replay those scenes as though you were already in the habit of walking gently in your world. Soak in the feelings you receive from making that change in your actions and responses.

Right now we can make the commitment to being more gentle. Living gently creates an aura of peace in our lives—a down comforter of support for ourselves and those with whom we are in relationships.

I live gently with myself and others.

I am a gentle and loving person.

I bring comfort to myself and others through my gentleness of spirit.

Jousting with
Our Inner Knight

ALTHOUGH WE'RE ALL ENDOWED WITH both feminine and masculine tendencies and talents, in western society the logical and linear masculine is seen as the more valuable. Unconsciously we often evaluate ourselves by society's standards and end up confused about what is worthwhile and appropriate within us. Our undervalued femininity, the bearer of intuition, wisdom, and empathy, feels the need to joust for place and power with our masculine inner knight, whose talents include getting the job done, empowerment, and motivation.

We need to integrate, not separate, the masculine and feminine aspects of our being. Through accepting and trusting both, we can help our inner knight free himself from his emotional armor as well as rescue our damsel from the dragon of victimization and weakness she has been subjected to by the narrow views of society. Synthesizing our varying, but equally valuable, feminine and masculine attributes and proficiencies creates balance, harmony, and wholeness.

Take a few silent minutes to effortlessly visualize your inner knight and lady. Are they able to work harmoniously with each other? If so, congratulate them and joyfully observe their dance. If not, encourage them to begin communicating with each other. What are their fears? What do they want and need from each other? How can they move toward sincere and lasting cooperation and mutual support? Don't expect miracles at first. Simply becoming aware of our feminine and masculine aspects and opening a dialogue between them is very healing.

The quest for mutually supportive relationships extends not only to those with whom we live, but also to those who live within us. By becoming acquainted with and accepting our differing parts, we can stop internal civil wars and learn to live as a productive, positive, and balanced whole person.

❧

*I love and admire both my feminine
and masculine attributes.*

I accept all parts of myself.

Flying toward the Flame

HAVE YOU EVER FELT AS THOUGH YOUR mind were filled with frantic moths fluttering around the flame of an insult or hurt? Try as we might to tame them, sometimes our thoughts insist on flying in and around the fire of our pain, and we end up feeling scorched by anger, guilt, or some other equally disturbing emotion.

During a fight with my husband in which I couldn't seem to get across to him why I was so angry, my thoughts were darting around in a frenzy. The drums they gyrated to were filled with fault-finding chants—*he should, I shouldn't, and if only!* I couldn't sleep and, because we were in a hotel room, also I couldn't go off by myself to do some calming meditation. I became more and more resentful as I lay there, exhausted, endlessly recounting my woes.

It wasn't until the very early morning hours that I began having the image of my thoughts as kamikaze moths determinedly flying toward the flame of my anger. With that valuable impression, I was able to begin calming my moths and cooling the flame, at least enough to allow me to drop off to sleep.

If you find yourself moth-minded, try this meditation. Close your eyes and conjure up a picture of your thoughts as moths. Allow yourself to see the flame of your resentment or anger and watch as your thoughts circle dangerously around it. Purposefully fan the flame and encourage it to burn even brighter. Watch as the flame licks and dances. Then very slowly and without judgment begin to deprive it of oxygen by putting something over it to snuff it out. As the flame quietly ceases to burn, gently gather up the moths and release them in a beautiful meadow filled with sweet-smelling flowers.

When we find our thoughts obsessively drawn into the flame of emotional pain, we need to consciously redirect them to a calming image or affirmation that encourages peace of mind. One of the most comforting statements I have used during such times is, "I can do all things through God who strengthens me."

I can change my thoughts.

I let go of anger and resentment easily.

Removing Thorns

IF WE GET A THORN IN OUR FINGER, our natural response is to pull it out—to eliminate the source of pain. Yet how many of us allow emotional thorns to embed themselves in us without ever acknowledging that we have the right to pull them out? Emotional thorns run the gamut from a relationship that is detrimental to our self-esteem to regret or guilt over something we did or that was done to us. Left unattended, emotional thorns can fester and acutely infect our attitudes.

Sherry, whose mother is an alcoholic, is a sad example of the damaging effects of unhealed emotional thorns. When Sherry was a child she mothered her mother and didn't receive the nurturance she needed and deserved. As an adult Sherry continued to care for her mom, but her feelings toward her turned to resentment and bitterness.

Although externally she did all the right things, internally the emotional thorn of her regret over her childhood experiences grew more and more poisonous to her daily life. Wisely, she sought counseling and learned to gently mother her inner child in ways that satisfied her longing. She plucked from her mind the primary sentences in her regret-litany and replaced them with self-valuing affirmations.

She also learned to set boundaries. Sherry's therapist once told her, "There is a statement in the Bible that goes something like this, 'You have the right to remove yourself from those who are vexations to your spirit.'" Today, she limits her caregiving of her mother to only that which she can do without resentment. She now supports herself when she is in need and encourages herself to remember that she has the right to remove emotional thorns.

Intuitively we know who and what is good for us. If we listen to ourselves with appreciation and trust our wisdom, rather than create judgments about our frailties, we'll know when it is healthy for us to remove our emotional thorns, and we'll give ourselves permission to do so.

❧

I encourage myself to heal.

I have the courage to remove painful emotional thorns.

Tilting at Disrespect

IN ORDER TO FEEL ACCEPTED AND supported by our environment, self-respect and the respect of others is essential. But many of us have not required others to treat us with respect and we often disrespect ourselves. To change this pattern, we need to cultivate a *pinball-machine* mentality and, when treated rudely or when overly jostled by demanding people including ourselves, go *tilt* and refuse to cooperate.

The first and most important step we can take toward a life characterized by respectfulness is to tilt at any disrespect we show *ourselves*. The habit of self-*dis*respect is not an easy one to break, but we can do it Gently and without recrimination, we need to observe our self-talk for signs of devaluing and blaming; then we can return to a supportive, no-fault attitude toward ourselves by creating self-talk that underscores and bolsters our self-respect. For instance, when we hear our inner voice saying something disrespectful such as "I can't do *anything* right," we need to stop and say, "Whoops, that's not true!" and alter the statement to a considerate one.

The same principle is true when we begin insisting on respect from others as well. If at work you are given responsibility without power or are expected to jump at the first scream from overly demanding and spoiled children or adults at home, ask yourself if you feel respected. If the answer is no, *tilt!* Since it's true that we teach people how to treat us, refusing to be treated shabbily is essential in earning the respect of others.

Although at first the people around us may be surprised by and resistant to our new call for respect, generally we'll ultimately receive the treatment we persist in requesting.

I deserve to be respected.

I respect myself.

I expect and insist that others treat me with respect.

Calming the Inner Sea

SO MUCH OF THE TURMOIL IN OUR LIVES is the result of our need to be right. Often we hold on to a grudge because we righteously know we're *right!* And maybe we are. But does that stubborn insistence that the other person acknowledge we are right add to our happiness or build a dam between us and him or her? Dr. Gerald Jampolsky, author of *Love Is Letting Go of Fear*, has a wonderful little statement that he tries to live by: *Would I rather be right or would I rather be happy?* I know which I choose—what about you?

It's difficult to give up the idea of being right because until we have an unshakable sense of our own worth, much of our security and self-esteem comes from believing we are right. But living with the attitude of *They better see it my way* or *I have to be right* leads to a stormy life filled with resentment.

I once had a couple in my therapy practice who had a heated argument over the habits of great white sharks. Each was sure they were right about certain details, and the more they tried to convince the other, the angrier they became. Finally, one turned to the other with a rueful grin and said, "Who the hell cares about sharks, anyway!" With that acknowledgment, they both began to laugh and the boiling emotional sea was calmed.

Calming our inner seas by deciding we would rather be happy than right doesn't mean that we acquiesce to others or relinquish our beliefs. It just means that we choose to let go of unimportant things that we have a stubborn tendency to gnaw on, terrier-like.

As Emmett Fox, the founder of Religious Science, says, "When you hold a resentment, you are bound to that person with a cosmic link." We want and need to be *connected* to others in supportive, loving ways, not bound to them by resentment, resistance, and the need to be right.

❦

I calm my inner sea by choosing to be happy.

I allow myself to float free of resentment.

*I love and accept myself when I am right
and when I am not.*

Traveling Tandem
and Flying Solo

SO MANY OF US HAVE TRAVELED TANDEM all of our lives; being intimately linked to others causes us, of necessity, to continually make compromises—conferring on everything from how to budget our money and where to live to what movie to see and what to eat for dinner. And generally we believe that the other person's desires, not ours, come first.

In order to flex our decision-making muscles, it's important to encourage ourselves to fly solo at least a few hours per week. We need time alone to recharge and to renew our ability to know what we want and to do what feels right for us—just us.

Priscilla had looked forward to a Saturday when her entire family was to be gone and she was to have the day to herself. But, instead of relaxing into the peace and quiet or energetically delving into a long-neglected hobby, she found herself wandering aimlessly around the house. About noon she came to the startling realization that her life had revolved around others' wants for so many years that she'd forgotten what she liked to do!

We have a responsibility to become the best person we can be, and we have the right to take enough time alone to reconnect with who that is. What are your likes, dislikes, desires, and talents? What are your goals? What unique gifts do you have to offer? By simply asking periodically, "What do *I* want to do? How do *I* feel now? What can *I* offer here?" we can flex our wings into responsible personal freedom.

Regularly flying solo renews our ability to be truly present to ourselves and, when we accept that it is all right for us to have time alone, we'll also be able to be more loving and receptive to the other people in our lives. Flying solo actually makes us a more compatible and compassionate tandem partner.

I make decisions easily.
I am entitled to solitude as well as togetherness.
I know what I want.

Dumping Dependence

IF WE CONTINUOUSLY LOOK TO OTHERS FOR our sense of safety, rely on them to make us feel worthwhile, and bank on their loving us to make us feel lovable, we are putting responsibility for the quality of our lives in someone else's hands. This makes us overly dependent, which is bad news for all concerned. In healthy relationships there is mutual *inter*dependence, but we need to dump dependence that is detrimental to our self-esteem and well-being.

Do we depend upon ourselves first for support, encouragement, and acceptance, or do we habitually cast about outside of ourselves, depending on others to provide these things for us? Of course there are times when it is natural and wise to seek reassurance from others; however, we need to be our own biggest boosters. We need a constant friend *inside* ourselves whom we can count on to encourage and nurture us no matter what the circumstance.

Allow your eyes to close gently and become as comfortable as you can. Imagine yourself in a beautiful, serene, and safe place. Quietly sink into the ambiance of this special location. Invite a presence that symbolizes your inner security to come and join you. It may appear as a person or as a symbol, such as an animal or a white light—any symbol is fine so long as you feel loved by it and in tune with it. Soak in the sensation of being protected by, and at one with, your inner security. Ask it how you can become better acquainted with it and be able to call on it confidently when you need it. Thank it for appearing to you, and let it know how much you appreciate it.

As we learn to have confidence in our inherent strength and accept it as an integral part of our higher selves, we will be able to dump overdependence on others and make room for mutually supportive interdependence.

I trust myself.

I am my own best expert.

I support myself unconditionally.

Cultivating Compassionate Detachment

DO YOU EVER FIND YOURSELF ACTING like an emotional vacuum cleaner, swooping into the corners of other people's pain and sucking it up as if it were your own? Although we may think this is the loving thing to do, it's not. It is important that we empathize—understand and comprehend another's feelings—but it is equally important that we try not to sympathize—allow others' feelings to affect us in a similar fashion. Sympathizing does not alleviate the other person's distress and it renders us less capable of being supportive, because we become swept away by our own feelings instead of able to concentrate on their experience.

An effective way to support others who are in pain is to cultivate compassionate detachment. Compassionate detachment asks that we feel deeply for another person, and understand the extent of her pain, without immersing ourselves in it or assuming responsibility to *solve it* or *make it better*. Compassionately paying attention to someone's distress is more constructive than attempting to *fix it*. Each person must find his or her own solutions, but being supported and encouraged along the way is a wonderful gift.

When I'm feeling pain that I can't understand, or if I realize I've vacuumed up someone else's pain, I find the following prayer very helpful: *Mother/Father God, if this is not my pain, I ask that it be taken to its perfect, right place and there be transformed and transmuted into the perfect, right energy. If it is my own pain, I ask for an understanding of its source. Thank You.*

Cultivating compassionate detachment frees us from "sympathy pains" and allows us to be truly involved with others by providing empathetic comfort, encouragement, and support.

I release all feelings that are not my own to their perfect conclusion.

I am a compassionate and empathetic person.

I care but do not carry.

Knitting the Raveled Sleeve

SLEEP, AS SHAKESPEARE SAID, KNITS UP the raveled sleeve of care. And who among us does not go to bed some nights with substantially raveled sleeves? We need our sleep because it replenishes all of our resources—emotional, physical, mental, and spiritual.

But just as an anorexic deprives her body of food, we sometimes starve ourselves of rest by attempting to sleep in an environment where we are overpowered by our partner's cover stealing, restlessness, or snoring.

Diane struggled out of bed each morning bleary-eyed and resentful, having spent yet another night unsuccessfully trying to block out the sound of her husband's snoring. By the time morning arrived, her nerves were frayed, her creativity dwindled, and her disposition soured. She almost hated him—the unwitting instrument of her torturous sleeplessness. When talking to Diane about her dilemma, I encouraged her to support herself by finding a comfortable place where she could sleep peacefully. With some guilt and trepidation, she mustered the courage to move into another bedroom.

Just recently she told me that the move had

saved her marriage. Watching Diane and her husband affectionately holding hands and laughing with one another, I could see the new relationship they had forged out of her willingness to take care of herself.

If our sleep vibrations do not mix and match well with our bed partner, this may sometimes mean we need a bedroom of our own. The sleep-on-the-couch cliché does not have to be a derogatory comment on the state of our relationship; rather it can mean that we have supported ourselves by creating a comfortable sanctuary, a feminine haven where we can get our much needed rest and knit up our raveled sleeve of care, undisturbed.

Sleeping well during the night means we are more likely to have an accepting and supportive attitude toward the people we meet during the day.

I sleep easily and peacefully.

I have the right to sleep in a comfortable, restful place.

Leaving Shame
and Guilt Behind

THE PERSON WE MOST OFTEN STAIN
with feelings of shame and guilt is ourself, and
much of our guilt and shame comes from believing we have failed in some way or other. Maybe
we "should" have been more successful, or
"shouldn't" have had an abortion, or "should"
have been able to stop his drinking. Some of us
can go on forever "should-ing" ourselves.

Mary Pickford, the actress, had a bit of insight on this subject I think we would be wise to
adopt. "If you have made mistakes . . . there is
always another chance for you. . . . You may
have a fresh start any moment you choose, for
this thing we call 'failure' is not the falling
down, but the staying down." Very few of us
stay down for long.

Sadie and Ashley, mother and daughter,
were talking about their past. Ashley told her
mom that she would tell her more about what
she was struggling with but didn't want Sadie to
feel guilty. Sadie wisely, and with hard-earned
self-love, said, "I'm over that. I see we were in
the same circumstances, but I didn't cause them.

If I'd had the power or the awareness, I would have changed the situation. I didn't have either, and I did the best I could." Don't we *all!*

Make a list of your seeming failures—the "shoulds" you think you need to feel shameful and guilty about. Ask yourself if you did the best you knew how at the time; if so, think of a symbolic way to release these feelings. For instance, a friend of mine gave me a jar labeled "Shoulds and Oughts." Periodically, I take out the little scraps of paper on which I have put my shame and guilt and burn them as a symbol of letting go and moving on.

Yesterday is irretrievable and tomorrow is unknown. We have done the best we could, and now it's time for us to forgive ourselves for our seeming failures, congratulate ourselves for getting up after falling down, and then leave remorse behind us.

I forgive myself for what I see as my past failures.

I deserve to be free of shame and guilt.

Accepting Our Former Selves

AS WE JOURNEY THROUGH LIFE, WE PLAY many parts; indeed we seem to be entirely different people at various ages. Some of those old selves may cause us to cringe with embarrassment and regret now, but a commitment to gain confidence and comfort ourselves necessitates moving back through the pages of our history and embracing those selves.

I had an experience that brought home to me how easily we hoard judgments against our earlier selves. Several years ago my former husband told me he had never been sexually attracted to me. He explained that he had always been captivated by small, petite brunettes. That's not me!

I was pained by his revelation but, more than that, relieved. I had always blamed my young married self totally for the failure of the marriage (after all, a woman worth her salt can keep a man, right?). But now I knew that I couldn't have changed my physical appearance.

In meditation, I invited the Sue I was in my twenties—uptight, French rolled, and unhappy—to come into my presence. Having always been a failure in my eyes, she came warily.

Greeting her in a new, more understanding way, I assured her that she had done all she could, that the marriage failure was neither hers nor her first husband's fault—they were too young and unable to be honest about what their needs were. Holding my young, former self in maternal, accepting arms, I asked her to forgive me for the blame I'd heaped on her all these years. She softened and seemed to become more confident as we both shed tears of reconciliation.

Take a quiet time to move back through the years and allow the image of an earlier self, one who needs your acceptance, to come into your mind. See the two of you enveloped in a clear and cleansing white light. Allow the light to flow through and around you both, healing any separation and bonding you together in love. From the wisdom of your current age, reach out and welcome that younger you into your heart.

❦

I accept my former selves.

I become a loving mother to my younger selves who need my forgiveness.

Developing Healthy Selfishness

THE FEAR OF APPEARING (OH, HORRORS!) selfish can lead us to give ourselves away until we are exhausted and drained absolutely dry. A dry well has nothing to offer to others. Cultivating selfishness can be a virtue that activates an ever-flowing spring of goodness from which we can share liberally with others.

It really is true that we do unto others as we do unto ourselves. Those who first love themselves are able to love others more genuinely. As we honor our own wants and needs, we can do the same for others. Those who truly love themselves—as opposed to being self-centered or self-absorbed—can trust, accept, and support others from a place of *I give freely* rather than *I need, therefore I give in hope of some return.*

Sit quietly and tune in to your breathing. Allow it to move as it will. After watching your breath for a few moments, encourage it to deepen. Take in new air from a loving universe and release used air to an accepting universe. See yourself, symbolically, as a vase—a vessel for sacred water. How full are you? If you are full to overflowing, you have much to offer the world. If you are less than full, your task is to *selfishly* fill your vessel. As you inhale, see your vase filling with crystalline water; as you exhale, let go of your old ideas about being selfish. Breathe and fill. Breathe and release.

Make a list of the things you would like to do for yourself but haven't because you thought it would be too selfish. If you do these things, will your life be richer? Will you be happier? Will you have more peace of mind? Will you be able to let go of some resentment? Will you feel more supportive of yourself? If you answered yes to any of these questions, your life and your relationships will benefit from the infusion of a little selfishness. So give yourself permission to be selfish!

*I have the right and the responsibility
to take care of myself.*

*I lift my vessel to Life and allow it
to fill to overflowing.*

I cultivate the virtue of healthy selfishness.

Finding Freedom
through Honest Feeling

*We should not pretend to understand the
world only by the intellect; we apprehend
it just as much by feeling.*

—Carl Jung

WE FREQUENTLY CATEGORIZE OUR feelings as good or bad, acceptable or unacceptable, and attempt to include only the good and acceptable ones in our lives. This usually doesn't work; because feelings are very often illogical and originate from old beliefs and experiences, they are not so easily managed.

Imagine that you have a galvanized tub—the apple-bobbing kind—filled with water and red and white Ping Pong balls. Let's pretend that someone has told you the red balls are bad and you need to keep them out of sight, below the surface of the water. How can you do it with just two hands? The only way I have come up with is to cut a piece of wood the size of the tub and hold down *all* of the balls—white and red alike. The same principle applies to our feelings. When we feel we have to submerge our "unacceptable" (by whose standards, I wonder?) feelings, we, of necessity, suppress others also. We become numb. Our lives lose their brilliance and excitement and we get confused about who we really are.

By becoming aware of our feelings, accepting them, and expressing them creatively and constructively, we free ourselves to be fully human.

Embracing Our Imperfections

WE GRANT OURSELVES AN IMMEASURABLE amount of freedom once we stop chastising ourselves because of our imperfections. Part of being human is to be less than perfect. This does not mean that we don't strive to be the best that we can be, but it does mean that we commit to being tolerant and supportive self-observers. With an encouraging inner perspective, we have a better chance of transforming our imperfections than with a hostile and judgmental attitude toward ourselves.

Many years ago when I was first learning the importance of loving myself, I met a man who taught me a very important shortcut to embracing imperfection. Cecil was a former Baptist minister whose father and grandfather had also been ministers. He described his family as a long line of perfect guilt carriers. In order to free himself from his belief that he had to be perfect, he regularly and good-humoredly shouted, "I made a mistake, so sue me!"

I took his motto as my own, and for years, when a less-than-perfect action or reaction overwhelmed me with feelings of shame, I would privately roar, "I made a mistake, so sue me!" Eventually, I began believing that I didn't have to be totally perfect all the time.

If we have been dedicated perfectionists for years, it will be difficult to embrace our imperfections, but it is possible. Not only can we learn to accept our peccadillos, but we can also begin to see them (providing they are relatively harmless) as rather likeable parts of our uniqueness.

Take a moment now to run a little movie in your mind with you and one of your self-proclaimed imperfections in the major roles. Step back from your critical feelings and view these players in a supportive light. Look at yourself and your idiosyncrasy as an unconditionally loving, doting grandmother might. Can you, with this understanding viewpoint, smile fondly and embrace yourself, imperfection and all? If not, try using another version of Cecil's motto: "I make mistakes, but I like and accept myself, anyway!"

I love and accept myself even though I am imperfect.
I accept myself unconditionally.

Integrating Anger

INTEGRATING ANGER INTO OUR LIVES IS crucially important to our sense of well-being. Since much of women's depression is actually suppressed anger, allowing ourselves to feel and healthily accept our anger helps keep us out of the doldrums of debilitating depression.

Marie was sixty-one before she was able to understand why she felt increasingly depressed and dependent on her husband and daughters. After reading several self-help books, she joined a support group. Listening to a group member read a poem about his painful childhood opened a door for Marie. Through this portal poured years of buried anger, fear, and anxiety based on a painful family history, beginning with her separation from her family at age two.

The older the feelings, the younger the inner child experiencing them. Because those internal little ones need safe arms to hold them as they move through pain toward healing, Marie was very wise to find a group to support her. As Marie went through the dark woods of her childhood into the light of her present life, she needed torch-bearers for the journey—as do we all.

Along with her group support Marie found, through the following exercise, an inner friend who also encouraged her. Using her dominant right hand, Marie wrote questions such as: Marie, you are ten years old, how do you feel? With her left hand she answered: I feel like crying. As her experiment progressed, Marie's right-hand messages became those of a compassionate mother figure and her left hand took on the role of her inner child, the bearer of unhealed feelings.

As we begin to integrate our anger, we need to remember that feeling angry is only a part of the process toward a heartfelt awareness that what caused the anger was then, and we are fully capable of changing and healing our lives now.

❦

I allow myself to be angry.

I move through anger into understanding and forgiveness.

I deserve to be supported as I move through difficult feelings.

Resting in Resistance

SO MANY OF US BELIEVE THAT WE NEED to resist our resistance, not let it "get the best of us." But resistance may be a message from our wise inner self to stop, listen, and pay attention.

When she moved to New York from California, Lindsey fully intended to continue her nursing career, but she found herself resisting it at every turn. For a while she caused herself a lot of emotional pain by berating herself for being too fearful or lazy to find a nursing position. Finally, wisely, she decided to pay careful attention to her resistance. She attempted to decipher her dreams, she began meditating on her inner protest against nursing, and she wrote her reflections in a journal. As she slowly started trusting her resistance, Lindsey began to understand how burned out she was on nursing and that she needed to take a sabbatical.

Author Stephen Levine talks about the *fist of resistance* with which we block out our pain—emotional or physical—and, thereby, create suffering. Resistance can magnify any pain into suffering. Conversely, allowing ourselves to truly feel our woundedness and then gently surrounding it with love and mercy helps diminish pain.

With your eyes closed, allow yourself to deepen your breathing. Sink into the rhythm of your breath moving in and out of your body. Invite yourself to relax. Very gently give yourself permission to explore a resistance you are experiencing now. Watch your reaction as you think of this resistance. Move your attention to your heart and shine a soft, warm light on it. Feel the suppleness of your heart and encourage it to soften even more. Now, with no pressure or *have to's*, encourage your heart to open to the resistance and allow mercy, love, and acceptance to flow toward it.

We can learn to rest in our resistance, lean into it gently, and send it love and mercy rather than battling or suppressing it. As we sensitively trust and explore our resistance, we'll be able to uncover the undoubtedly wise *reason* for it.

❧

I explore my resistance and, consequently, learn from it.

I know what is good for me.

Remembering to Breathe

ONE OF THE BEST WAYS TO FREE OUR feelings is to breathe into them. Deep breathing assists us in several crucial ways. Physically, it cleanses our body of air that has been sapped of life-giving oxygen, replacing it with fresh, rejuvenating air. Interestingly, studies show that when elderly people practice deep breathing for only a few minutes a day, their memories improve dramatically.

Psychologically, slow, deliberate, deep breathing allows us to move below surface feelings into an awareness of causal, root emotions that may be breeding discomfort in our lives. Spiritually, deep breathing connects us to the flow of God's universe and anchors us firmly in our center, bringing us a sense of calm.

Yet, especially when we're tense or in crisis, we literally forget to breathe. This puts us in the position of attempting to cope while being deprived of vital oxygen. Very difficult to do.

Do yourself a life-enhancing favor. Remember to breathe deeply. Write a little note that says simply, *Breathe*, and refer to it several times a day, especially when you need to be sharp and at your best.

For years I was an amateur actress, and for many of those years I suffered from acute stage fright. To overcome the fear I learned a simple yoga exercise to do before going on stage. It included *breathing* and saying, "I'm glad you're here, I'm glad I'm here, and I know that I know!" I now do that same exercise when I speak in public. It makes a world of difference.

Practice breathing deeply for a few minutes right now. Arrange your body in a comfortable position and gently allow your breath to deepen, breathing in through your nose and out through your mouth. Imagine your body hungrily receiving these sustaining breaths and gratefully releasing its stale air. Thank your breath for its unfailing service to you.

The beautiful thing about remembering to breathe deeply is that we can do it anywhere, in any situation. It is guaranteed to improve things!

I am thankful for my breath.

In times of crisis I remember to breathe deeply.

Answering "Present!"

FEELING BORED OR OVERWHELMED MAY mean that we are approaching life like an apathetic teenager going to school—not present with enthusiasm but rather attending in a fog of indifference. If we play hooky from life by automatically doing what has to be done but savoring nothing, we're robbing ourselves of the chance to vigorously *feel* and *live* life. We are not answering "Present!" when Life calls the roll.

In order to feel vitally alive and live up to our creative potential, we need to make a commitment to being present in our lives, up front and *paying* attention, not just slumped in the back row apathetically waiting for the bell to ring.

Brittany was considering dropping out of college because she felt it was boring, useless, and too much work. Underneath those feelings was a sense of failure and futility over her low grades. A fellow student shared with Brittany a tip she had gotten from a study video called "Where There's a Will, There's an A": *Sit in the front row in all classes.* Not totally trusting such a simple solution but wanting to succeed, Brittany decided to try.

She was uncomfortable at first, but soon she began to look forward to getting to classes early in order to ensure herself a seat up front. Instructors who had seemed aloof and dull now often talked directly to her and recognized her on campus. Her enthusiasm for her courses took an astounding forward leap and, at the end of the semester, her grades reflected her interest.

Encouraging ourselves to sit in the front row of life invites us to be attentive to and appreciative of all its varied aspects. When we answer, "Present!" we'll be rewarded by *conscious* living in which we are aware of our feelings, rather than separated from them.

❦

I give myself the gift of sitting up front in my life.

I pay attention.

I have a right to really experience my feelings.

Mining the Gold of Dreams

OUR DREAMS ARE A GOLD MINE OF information. Not only do they siphon off excess energy and anxiety, but they can also inspire and educate us. Dreams give us a glimpse into both our subconscious and unconscious minds and allow us to access parts of ourselves often veiled in the glare of daily existence. Dreams are movies in which we are the sole director, actor, producer, and creator; yet, how often do we intentionally attend these movies and allow ourselves to be entertained and enlightened?

Julia, a client of mine, was vaguely discontent but couldn't understand why. We explored one of her dreams in which she was hospitalized and unwillingly subjected to many procedures. In the dream she felt powerless to voice her opinion. Everyone else seemed to know what was good for her and would not listen to any of her suggestions.

Exploring this dream gave Julia nugget after nugget of insight about her lifelong habit of allowing others to make her choices for her. By recognizing her tendency to unquestioningly comply with others, she saw that a large part of her unhappiness stemmed from feeling power-less in her marriage. Using her dream as an indi-cator of her feelings, Julia worked on expressing herself and stating her preferences. Slowly she gained the confidence to make her own deci-sions and speak up for herself. In the process of owning her power, her listlessness diminished and she began feeling happier.

A good way to tap into the wisdom of your dreams is to keep a pen and paper by your bed. Immediately after you wake up, replay the dream and then jot down some shorthand notes that will help you reclaim the dream. Later, you can go back and fill in the details.

Spend time with your dreams. Rerun them. Symbolically take the pickax of your intuition into the gold mine of your dreams, knowing that their meaning will be revealed to you as you take the time to mine the treasure.

I easily remember my dreams.

*I enjoy studying my dreams and
readily interpret them.*

Ringing True

ANNE FRANK, WHO WAS WISE BEYOND her years, said, "Everyone has inside him a piece of the good news. The good news is that you don't know how great you can be! How much you can love! What you can accomplish! And what your potential is!" In her brief time, Anne nourished and expressed her authentic self through introspection and writing and, consequently, has posthumously touched and inspired countless hearts.

One of our most important tasks is to recognize in ourselves what Anne Frank terms "the good news." How great can we be? How much love are we capable of giving? What accomplishments wait to be achieved? What vast potential beckons? Only through feeding our authenticity will we be able to fully dramatize our good news, our potential, our gifts to the world.

Feeding our authenticity consists of many things, including being aware of and honoring our true feelings, accepting ourselves totally, listening to our inner voice, supporting and encouraging ourselves, comforting and nurturing ourselves, giving ourselves permission to act independently, accepting help when we need it, and making space for solitude and creativity.

Being true to ourselves is the most important way we can feed our authenticity. Take a few minutes now to quietly tune into yourself. Gently feel yourself sinking into the center of your being. Block out distractions to the best of your ability, and give yourself your undivided attention. Allow your breathing to deepen. Inhale slowly through your nose and exhale slowly through your mouth.

Bring into your mind's eye an image of yourself as a beautiful bell in a steeple. If the bell you first sense doesn't please you, change it until both its sight and sound are uplifting to you. Listen with love, acceptance, and admiration as your bell melodiously peals out the good news of your authenticity.

If our steeple bell—the unique and authentic self at the center of our being—is to chime and charm the entire valley of which we are a part, then it must ring true!

❦

I accept the good news that I am great.

I am true to myself.

Becoming an
Inner Environmentalist

WE ARE BECOMING MORE RESPONSIBLE FOR our planet by adopting environmentally conscious ways of living on Mother Earth in the fervent hope that she will thrive and continue to support us. But equally important to our lives is an increased awareness of the detrimental consequences of inner pollution, caused by self-condemnation, unsupportive relationships, exhausting schedules, unhealed emotional wounds, and a lack of spiritual conviction.

If we are to feel comforted rather than criticized and encouraged rather than futile, we must become an inner environmentalist, cleaning out unwanted feelings and clearing a space for health and wholeness. If your inner pain is deep-seated and of long standing, resulting from such traumatic experiences as incest or child abuse, please do not try to handle it alone. Find a therapist or friend who can compassionately and tolerantly stand by you as you courageously sort, discard, and heal unwanted feelings that are polluting your life.

As a small step toward cleaning and clearing,

visualize your inner environment as a garage. Is it cluttered with the debris of old pain, impossible expectations, and devaluing assumptions? Is it polluted by the stench of resentment, envy, or self-condemnation? If so, begin to take out the trash! In your mind's eye, dispose of unwanted and outdated emotional rubbish in ways that feel the most freeing to you, even to the point of tearing down and rebuilding the entire garage if that seems to be the right thing to do. When you've finished, survey the newly cleaned or reconstructed garage and savor the order you have restored to it.

No matter where our emotional garbage originated, it is our responsibility now to discard it, heal it, and free ourselves from it. It is possible, with commitment and courage, to become happy, healthy, and emotionally uncluttered.

I have the courage to face and cleanse
my inner pollution.

I ask for encouragement and support when I need it.

Removing the Cauldron
from the Fire

FROM TIME TO TIME, WE FIND OURSELVES embroiled in a cauldron of discontent, stewing over things we wish were different. When this happens, we can *choose* to remove the cauldron from the fire by changing our focus to action rather than reaction. For when we allow our cauldron of negative feelings to remain too long in the fire, we become hard-boiled.

One day, when all four of my kids were still at home, I was preparing dinner in a fit of resentment. Good grief!—one of them could almost always be counted on to turn up a nose at the meal I'd cooked. I stomped around the kitchen wondering why I had to prepare all the meals. I added more worms and spiders' eyes to my bitch's brew by chastising myself for not having the guts to *demand* more help. My victimized self-talk had just gotten my internal cauldron almost to the boiling point when I glanced at a little saying stenciled on my recipe box: Lord, help me add a dash of love!

That saying stopped me in my tracks. It certainly wasn't love—either for myself or for my family—that I'd been adding to the dinner. What could I do to remove my cauldron from the fire and be able to honestly add a dash of love when I cooked? For me, the most important realization was how angry I felt over being the only cook. With that understanding, I was able to change my focus from resentment to possible solutions, including initiating a cook's night off at least once a week.

Gently center yourself in whatever way works for you, and allow to float into your mind a situation that causes your internal cauldron to boil. What angers you or causes you resentment? Have you allowed yourself to feel victimized by the circumstances? What dash of love *toward yourself* do you need to add to the equation in order to start changing the situation? Gently assure yourself that you have the right and responsibility to transform these feelings, and commit to supporting yourself in removing your cauldron from the fire.

I have the courage to be assertive.
I listen to my feelings and act on them
when appropriate.

Letting the Shadow Roam

ACCORDING TO CARL JUNG, THE SHADOW parts of ourselves are undeveloped or denied aspects of our beings that need to be acknowledged. If we were brought up to be "nice" girls, for example, we were probably also taught to be ashamed of our shadow—our rage, assertiveness, ambition, sexuality, even our creativeness—denying and repressing it to the detriment of our well-being.

Denied, our shadow gains strength and becomes almost diabolical in its ability to cause us, and others, pain. But when we embrace our shadowy aspects and learn to express them in *constructive* ways, their energy is transformed and, therefore, able to merge in a healthy way with our other parts.

When Allie discovered that her husband was having an affair, her immediate desire was to kill both him and the woman. Terrified by her reaction, she quickly quelled that very natural shadow response and instead began feeling that it was her fault he had strayed. She became increasingly depressed until she could hardly move from the couch. She eventually dragged herself to see me.

It required a lot of encouragement from me for Allie to face her shadow. Beneath her depression she was boiling with rage, the power of which absolutely petrified her. When she was finally satisfied that it was okay to have such emotions, but that they needed to be acted on *constructively*, she began letting her shadow roam. She threw eggs at trees and wrote volumes of hate letters to her betrayers and then burned them.

Most important, Allie stopped judging herself for her emotions and began to really feel empowered by her shadow. In the process, she realized that her biggest contribution to the cracking of her marriage had been her inability to be her own person. Although it has been a long and difficult road, happily, Allie and her husband are in the process of creating a new, healthier marriage.

Like the dark side of the moon, our shadow is ever present. It is up to us to liberate and illuminate it.

❦

I am a nice person even though I have ugly feelings.

I invite my shadow out to play.

Melting Stress through Motion

LAKES OR PONDS FED BY MOVING WATER remain fresh and clear. Similarly, by encouraging ourselves to *move*, we can transform unwanted emotional stagnation into vitality. Putting ourselves *in motion* can help us achieve the e-motions we would like to have.

Physically, movement facilitates circulation and helps the body process the nutrients it needs; mentally, putting the body into action helps us clear out the cobwebs and makes us sharper. Feeling better physically and keener mentally, in and of itself, makes our emotions more harmonious. We just plain feel better about ourselves when we move.

Different types of motion serve different purposes. Yoga and Tai Chi are meditative practices that are excellent physical disciplines as well as being useful for centering, calming, and comforting ourselves. Martial arts help us hone our bodies and our minds. Walking, biking, and aerobic dance are wonderful for reducing stress and tension.

Carla, a special-education teacher, tries never to miss her three-times-a-week aerobic class. She uses it for both physical and emotional fitness. If she has had a sad or frustrating experience with one of her students, a parent, or the administration, she puts her objects of anger in front of her and pretends to punch them each time she moves. As she visualizes the culprits reeling from her cuffing, she can feel her stress and tension melting away.

Encourage yourself to get up and move right now. We still have within us that spontaneous child who intuitively knows how to *dance toward balance and harmony*. Invite her out to play. Let her remind you of the transformative value of unrehearsed motion.

I enjoy being in motion.

I choose the form of exercise and movement that is right for me and commit to doing it.

I allow my inner child to dance and play spontaneously.

Accepting What Is

I find that it is not the circumstances in which we are placed, but the spirit in which we meet them that constitutes our comfort.

—Elizabeth King

WHEN WE CAN ADOPT THE following simple but profound prayer as our life's creed, we epitomize acceptance in its healthiest form: *God, grant me the serenity to accept the things I cannot change, the courage to change the things I can, and the wisdom to know the difference.*

Acceptance is a difficult lesson to learn. There are always conditions in our lives over which we have no control, and we can get stuck believing that circumstances should be a certain way in order to be acceptable, or that people must act in a prescribed fashion before we can find them acceptable. Caught in the intolerance of our *shoulds* and *have to's*, acceptance is canceled out. When we clutch resistance tightly to our chests and vow we'll never accept thus and so, we cement ourselves into the situation, attitude, or pain.

The acceptance I am talking about is not giving up or lapsing into hopeless resignation; it is having the wisdom to know when to say, "Ah, this is how it is. How can I have peace of mind in the face of this?"

Kicking the Approval Habit

ONE OF THE MOST INSIDIOUS ADDICTIONS we women struggle with is our craving for approval from others. When our need for validation gets in the way of our being who we truly are, we're in trouble. Fueled by a belief that we need *their* approval in order to be okay, we scurry around looking for "self"-esteem fixes from suppliers that are outside of ourselves. It doesn't work.

Of course we all need people to appreciate us, but our primary source of approval needs to come from ourselves. The very best way to kick the approval habit is to support and approve of ourselves. This doesn't mean that we overlook our shortcomings or pat ourselves on the back for being nasty, but, in my many years of being a psychotherapist, I have seen very few people who err on the side of being too *easy* on themselves.

Authentic self-approval naturally leads to increased approval of others. Malia attracts friends like flowers attract bees. She is a heartlifter; around her everyone feels better about themselves. She always seems to have a sincere word of praise for those around her.

But others are not the only recipients of her approval. She is also very self-confident and comfortable about bestowing accolades on herself. It's not unusual for her, in an unaffected and honest way, to say something like, "I am so proud of the way I handled that!" Asked if she had always been so kind to herself, she giggled, "Oh no, I used to be my own worst enemy, but I learned to be my own best friend instead!"

When we learn to accept who we are right now and celebrate who we are becoming, we can kick the approval habit and rely on ourselves for our best approval *fixes*.

I wholeheartedly approve of myself right now.

What others think of me is their choice;
what I think of me is my choice.

I easily approve of others.

Viewing Discipline
As Desirable

ACCEPTING THE FACT THAT WE ARE responsible for our own lives is incredibly empowering. We may have been erroneously taught that we were in charge of making other people's lives happier, but few women have been encouraged to see that, in reality, we are responsible for making our *own* lives work. Accepting that "the buck stops here" so far as responsibility for our attitudes and accomplishments is concerned requires self-confidence—the awareness that we are capable and can do it, whatever *it* is at the moment.

If we are to maintain confidence in ourselves, we must be able to trust that we'll do what we say we're going to do. This requires a healthy amount of self-discipline—not the harsh and strict expectations a critical parent might have, but reasonable and *do-able* self-discipline—such as setting realistic goals and then following through with what we have agreed to do.

Although the word *discipline* sometimes evokes a negative response, it actually comes from the word *disciple,* meaning a learner who is in loving response to a respected teacher. Viewing ourselves as both a teacher and a learner simultaneously, not as an errant child in need of punishment, helps us do whatever needs doing.

During a quiet time when you will not be disturbed, allow yourself to focus on your breathing. Effortlessly deepen your breathing, relaxing more completely with each inhalation and exhalation. In this relaxed state, gently allow a sense or picture of a loving and respected teacher to come into your awareness. If the person or symbol that appears is not totally comfortable for you, ask it to leave and invite the perfect teacher to appear.

Take a few minutes to simply *be* with your teacher, basking in love and acceptance. Then discuss with your teacher an attitude or circumstance about which you are having difficulty being disciplined. Ask for assistance. Together, you will know how to create an environment where the needed discipline can blossom.

❧

I enjoy being gently self-disciplined.
I accept responsibility for my life.

Sitting with "I Don't Know"

ENDURING THE UNKNOWN IS DRAINING for most of us. Whether it is waiting for the results of a test, wondering about the outcome of a job interview, or questioning whether a particular relationship is healthy for us, we have a tendency to want the answer *now*. Especially difficult is having the patience and wisdom to allow our inner sorting process to happen naturally—sitting with our "I don't know"—rather than forcing ourselves into decisions and commitments before we really *know* what is best.

Just as babies take months to develop and seeds take days or weeks to sprout, most of our answers unfold from an internal questioning period in which the only honest and authentic reality *is* "I don't know." Our task is to accept this process as creative and productive, honor and embrace our questions, and trust that, if we allow it, the best choice will eventually evolve.

After moving to a new state, my husband and I were having difficulty finding a home we both liked. I found my dream spot, four acres with a gorgeous view, but Gene realized that four acres would require more work than either of us wanted to do. He then found what appeared to be a fair compromise, but I couldn't get excited about the new site. Having been a dedicated husband-pleaser for many years, it took a lot of courage for me to sit with my "I don't know" about the property. I wasn't sure if my resistance was intuition about what was right for us or rebellion over not getting the acreage I loved.

It would have been easy for me to capitulate and do what I felt Gene wanted, but I sat with the issue, sifting and sorting the pros and cons until I *knew*: the site was not for me. Luckily, a few patient weeks later, we found a lot that we *both* loved.

Although sitting with our "I don't knows" may feel like an endless free-fall, it allows our astute interior computer to gather the information necessary to make valid decisions.

I trust myself to make good decisions.

I honor my questions and patiently pursue my own answers.

Letting Go through Ritual

MANY UNACCEPTABLE THINGS HAPPEN to us in a lifetime. Paradoxically, in order to live life to the fullest, we must learn to accept *all* of life's incidents—the wonderful and the terrible. Accepting the unacceptable is so foreign and repulsive to our conscious mind that we often need to bypass it, through ritual, in order to impress our subconscious mind with our intention toward acceptance.

As a result of a routine mammogram, Frances found herself diagnosed, hospitalized, and without a breast before she was able to process her feelings let alone accept the unacceptable fact of having cancer. During her convalescence, Frances ran the emotional gamut from thankfulness for her life to despair over her appearance and the possible recurrence of the disease.

Dedicated to healing physically and emotionally, Frances decided to plan a letting-go ritual. She wanted to commemorate not only the loss of her breast, but all of the things she regretted losing or never having during her fifty years. After gathering pictures of herself that were representative of her regrets, she burned them in the backyard. Frances visualized the fire transforming those images of hurt, pain, and loss into more positive energy. To conclude, Frances buried the ashes and ceremoniously celebrated communion with herself as she watched the twilight deepen.

Scan your mind and feelings for anything you have not yet been able to accept. Ask yourself if you are honestly willing to let go of the pain and move on. If your answer is no, honor that—the time may not be right. But if you feel ready to release the pain, create a ritual for yourself that will notify your subconscious of the decision. When you sincerely wish to heal through ritual, the perfect way to do so will occur to you.

Accepting what is, even though it's not what we wish it to be, is letting go of all hope of a better yesterday. And that allows us to fully embrace today as it is.

I give myself the gift of letting go of
the unchangeable past.

I use ritual to heal the deepest parts of myself.

I am wise.

Accepting Who We Are

TO ACCEPT WHO WE ARE AND WHO WE are not is a fundamental invitation being issued continually from our higher selves. What a challenge! It is such a temptation to "if only" our acceptance to death: If only I were more successful . . . If only I were married (or single) . . . If only I were smarter, prettier, wiser . . . then I would be able to accept myself.

Because during our lifetime we are involved in a continual reincarnation of selves—being reborn regularly into new identities, new beliefs, new talents—it is imperative that we learn to accept ourselves *now*, as is. We may never get another chance to accept the self who looks back from the mirror today. By tomorrow she may be an entirely new person. If we accept her today, that new woman will be happier and more capable than the one who lives in our skin now.

My mother was a wise and talented woman who had a unique gift for listening intently and caring deeply for people. Yet she struggled her entire life to accept herself. I knew how many lives, including mine, she had touched in a loving way, and watching her wrestle with the demon of low self-esteem broke my heart. Because of her inability to accept herself as the truly wonderful person she was, Mother wondered, especially in the last months, if her life had been meaningful. Reassurances assuaged her doubts for a while, but they always returned.

The extent of her effect on people was underscored by the length of her funeral caravan winding its way to the cemetery. On the ride, I said silently to her, "Do you see those cars, Mom? Now can you accept and believe how wonderful you are?" The message I got back was filled with chuckles and exuberance and said, "Yes, Honey, you were right . . . *now* I can see it!"

Let us not wait until tomorrow—or eternity—to accept who we are. Let's do it right now.

❦

I deserve acceptance from myself and others.

I am acceptable just as I am.

I accept myself.

Making Sacrifices

IN BOOKS AIMED AT HELPING WOMEN learn to empower themselves, we are often warned about habitual self-sacrifice, but there are times when sacrificing individual desires is a valid way to honor who we truly are. In family crises, such as illness or loss of income, sacrificing our personal needs for the good of the whole is often the most appropriate and satisfying thing we can do.

Josie, an artist, is a good example of a woman who knows how to distinguish between appropriate and inappropriate service. For many years, her husband suffered from chronic kidney failure. Josie put her art, as well as her needs, on the back burner in order to care for her husband. Since she freely *chose* to make her husband and his health the priority, she experienced no resentment. In fact, because she revelled so much in his talent, sense of humor, and searching intellect, she felt she gained as much as she gave. Every day of her life Josie sacrificed and felt good about herself while doing so.

Six years ago Josie's husband died, and since then she has made a very conscious choice *not* to sacrifice for others but to put her own talents, wants, and needs on the front burner of her life. And that is the perfect choice for her now.

Our feelings are the most legitimate indicators of whether the sacrifices we're making are appropriate or inappropriate. If, for the most part, we feel good about our actions and decisions, it probably means that our sacrifice springs from *wanting* to serve. If, however, we consistently experience such feelings as anxiety, resentment, or anger, our sacrifice may come from believing we have no other option.

If you are feeling used and abused while sacrificing, it is important to find someone with whom you can talk freely. The right listener can help you explore your feelings, attitudes, and options. As women who have historically been designated the care-givers, our big challenge is knowing when our inclination toward sacrifice and service is appropriate and when it is not.

❦

I make wise choices.

When necessary and appropriate, I sacrifice from a full and loving heart.

Riding in the Change Parade

OUR LIVES ARE A CONSTANT PARADE OF changes! Some will be inspiring and exciting, making us want to grab our baton, jump in front of the band, and shout for joy. Others will more closely resemble a funeral cortege. In light of its inevitability, befriending change is a comforting philosophy for us to work toward. By looking for the personal growth inherent in any new phase of life, we can make the Change Parade work *for* us rather than against us.

Doggedly resisting change sets us up to be forever fighting the inescapable, which can eventually lead to feelings of hopelessness and depression. When we master the art of accepting change and commit to making the best of it, we are choosing to evolve—to be vital, useful, and happier people.

I recently read an inspiring story about a courageous teenager from whom we can learn a lot about assimilating change. Sixteen-year-old cancer patient Beth was given two choices: radiate the tumor and hope the cancer would die, or amputate her foot and keep the disease from spreading. Beth made the decision to "take it off." While her optimistic outlook faltered when she saw the stump for the first time, one day the crying stopped and, as Homecoming Princess, she hobbled out onto the field in her cheerleading outfit to admiring applause from the crowd.

In the Change Parade of her young life, Beth not only *walked* on her new artificial foot but, a year and a half after surgery, she—and the eleven other members of her squad—twirled, scissor-kicked, jumped, and danced her way to a Class A State Cheerleading Championship.

When Beth was asked what she had learned, she answered, "You can take any situation and make it better by bringing yourself up." As Beth's courageous acceptance of her situation shows, the Grand Marshall in the Change Parade of our lives is often greater courage and expanded compassion. You too can bring yourself up!

I have the courage to accept change.

I allow change to teach me valuable lessons.

Making It through the Rain

WE ALL KNOW, OR KNOW OF, INSPIRING people who seem to weather life's greatest storms in the most growth-producing ways. Leslie, a single mother, is such a person. At thirty-two she was stricken with a rare and usually fatal form of cancer. When first diagnosed, she was panic stricken and enraged, bereft at the thought of not seeing her daughter grow up. Understandably, she sank into a depression.

As Leslie puts it, one day she *awoke* from her depression with the awareness that her life force, or life flame as she calls it, was not yet extinguished. In that illuminating moment, she realized that it was up to her to protect her life flame from this life-threatening deluge. She began to meditate regularly, and at length, on the light in each cell of her body—even the cancer cells—centering on transforming the cancer cells rather than destroying them.

Leslie supported her life force by learning to love and appreciate herself exactly as she *was*, and then concentrated on transforming the destructive cells with the light of love. Hope and faith became Leslie's slicker in this storm, and self-acceptance and understanding were the umbrellas protecting her flickering life flame.

When faced with almost certain death, Leslie realized how desperately she wanted to learn to lovingly accept herself and her family in ways she hadn't been able to before. With that goal in mind, Leslie did make it through the rain. Today she is healthy, but she says that so sincere was her acceptance of herself and her illness, that she would have been at peace even if death had been the outcome.

Into each life a little rain must fall. All of us will experience storms during our lifetime, and we all have the inner strength and wisdom to weather them with grace. We can make it through the rains more easily when we greet them protected by self-love, acceptance, and support.

❀❀

I lovingly accept myself.

I weather the storms of life gracefully.

I learn to better understand myself during stormy times.

Changing What Can
Be Changed

You may be disappointed if you fail, but you're doomed if you don't try.

—*Beverly Sills*

IMAGINE WHAT IT WOULD BE LIKE IF the owner of an aquarium never changed the water in the tank. It wouldn't be long before the fish died attempting to glean oxygen from a stagnant and used-up source. Changing the water and keeping it circulating allows marine animals to thrive in their habitat. It's much the same with us. Without change we would stagnate.

Although many of us resist it fiercely, change forces us to grow and evolve, to become more flexible, resilient, and confident. Our task is to transcend any fear of the unknown and encourage ourselves to change what needs to be different in our lives in order for them to flow freely and creatively.

A wonderful Zen story tells of a teacher giving a student a silk scarf snarled in many knots. The student's assignment was to free the scarf of the knots, a chore he struggled with until receiving the insight that, in order to succeed, he must untie the knots in reverse order.

Change can be difficult, but when we trust ourselves to untie each little knot, in the right order, our entire scarf can eventually be freed to flutter gently in the breeze.

Knowing We Are in Charge
of Our Attitudes

IN THE FACE OF UNCOMFORTABLE circumstances, sometimes the only thing we have the power to change is our mind. During times when we feel out of control, we can comfort ourselves by remembering, as the Reverend June Kelly says, "We are the *only* author of our thoughts—the only thinker in our lives." *We* are in charge of our attitudes. Since feelings are a direct result of attitudes and thoughts, the ability to change our minds is one of our most precious and useful attributes.

Society encourages us to be what it considers *realistic,* and there are even semiderisive descriptions for those people with positive attitudes: cockeyed optimist, Pollyanna, and ivory-tower idealist to name a few. But why is it cockeyed to be optimistic? Why isn't a tendency to expect the best possible outcome wise, rather than naive or stupid?

A dedicated realist might answer that we are only setting ourselves up for disappointment when we habitually expect the best; I would respond by saying that a negative or pessimistic attitude, masquerading as realism, ensures us discouragement as we apprehensively wait for the ax to fall.

Ariel graduated from college two years ago and, following a successful internship, went out to find a job. Many realists presented her with grim statistics on the limited market for her skills. At first she felt almost paralyzed with discouragement.

A good talk with her mother helped Ariel realize she needed to change her attitude, focusing instead on how fortunate any company would be to have her as an employee. When pessimism crept in during particularly frustrating periods in her job search, Ariel reassured herself by choosing to remember what she had to give, rather than concentrating on what she feared she had to lose. Although it took a while, Ariel is now employed full-time in her field.

Knowing we are in charge of our attitudes is one of the most life-enhancing realizations we can come to.

❦

I am an optimist and proud of it.
I choose to expect the best.

Reframing Reality

THERE ARE THOSE OF US WHO SEE REALITY only by the harsh glare of television news coverage or in the unknowable shadows of "what if...." Because the news seems to accentuate the negative, and the unknown is often so frightening, is it any wonder that one of our society's primary diseases is depression?

But the good news is that we can reframe reality. We can choose what we look at, listen to, and respond to. Yes, negative things happen. Yes, there is much pain and suffering—in the world and in our own lives—and we need to have compassion for it. But we don't have to become irretrievably entangled in it to the detriment of our own happiness. The French novelist Colette summed up this choice when she said, "What a wonderful life I've had. I only wish I'd realized it sooner."

We can realize how wonderful our lives are by changing what we focus on—how we frame our reality. An elderly friend of mine said that calling herself a housewife didn't seem to command the respect she felt it deserved so she changed her title. When asked what she did, she responded that she was a social arbitrator.

Not only did others seem more impressed by her career choice, but *she* believed it to be a much fairer description of her role and therefore felt more valued.

Quietly think of a situation in your life that you consider difficult or depressing. Allow your creative mind to take a snapshot of it. Now bring into your awareness the frame that you have this situation in. Is it dark and heavy? Huge and cumbersome? Covered with ugly decorations? Ask yourself how you would like to frame this situation. Allow a new frame to appear, one more manageable and maybe even beautiful. What change in attitude will you need in order to reframe your picture? When this situation next arises, take a moment to see it in the context of your new frame.

As we learn to reframe our reality, our lives can become filled with the fantastic, heaped with heroes, and loaded with love.

❦

I choose to see how wonderful my life is.

I have the power to reframe my reality.

I appreciate my life and all its variations.

Facing the Fork in the Road

WHILE STANDING AT A FORK IN THE ROAD, wondering what choice to make, it is important to take into account what is really right for us. So many of us women almost automatically say, "Whatever *you* want," as we stand on the threshold of a decision. Such self-denying, and often unconscious, behavior can cover the spectrum from a simple acquiescence, such as not choosing a restaurant, to a major sacrifice, such as giving up a career because someone else disapproves or may be inconvenienced.

Perhaps at a crossroad in our lives we disowned an important dream, ignored the yearning of our hearts, or simply did not do for ourselves what we would automatically have done for a friend. Regrets are born from the resultant feelings of self-betrayal.

Sit quietly for a few minutes and focus entirely on your breathing. If your mind wanders, as it probably will, very gently return your attention to your breath, gradually allowing it to deepen. With each inhalation, sense your body's gratitude for this clean air. As you exhale, feel yourself relaxing. Invite into your mind's theater a circumstance in your life that feels like a fork in the road. Carefully observe how you feel and act when faced with the decision of which path to follow. Explore your fears, expectations, and hopes concerning each road. Quietly ask yourself what route is best for you. If your answer is a quagmire of contradictions, concentrate on your breath once again until you feel relaxed.

After recentering yourself, write the question: What is the right decision for me in this instance? Jot down your first thought. Follow that with the simple question, Why? and list your reasons, to help affirm your choice. We *know* what is best for us and when we allow ourselves to really listen to our inner wisdom, we can turn a fork in the road into a genesis of self-respect and self-esteem.

❧

I have the strength to handle the consequences and the rewards of my choices.

I know what is best for me and act accordingly.

Defibrillating Our Funny Bone

IF WE DISCOVER THAT RESPONSIBILITY and seriousness have shuttled our sense of humor off into cold storage, where it has atrophied from lack of use, we can rescue and revive it. We have the power to decide to change our outlook—lighten it up, let it bubble rather than grumble.

Sometimes our funny bone, as well as our zest for life, gets buried under fear of ridicule or disillusionment. Hilary, whose mother often cautioned her against getting too excited about anything for fear she would be disappointed, is a good example of entombed enthusiasm. Having been disappointed often in her own life, Hilary's mother felt she was doing her daughter a favor by saving her from the same grief she had experienced. As she grew up, Hilary took her mother's advice and tightly controlled her emotions and anticipations until her life felt flat and leveled. Safe, but dull and joyless.

Feeling that life must hold more passion than this, Hilary decided she wanted to defibrillate her funny bone and invite humor and excitement back into her life. As an affirmation, she purchased a personalized license plate that says

GTXCITD. Each time Hilary sees her car she's reminded that it's all right—and even much healthier—to *get excited.*

Even if we have temporarily forgotten that life can be pretty darned funny a lot of the time, we can *choose* to remember to take everything less seriously, patch our levity leaks, and let laughter lighten our load. Humor and enthusiasm are *natural!* If we're not experiencing them it's because we have buried our inherent impulse to *play.*

It might help to find a symbol of playfulness—a picture, a balloon, a clown pin, a puppy or unicorn sticker, whatever—and carry it with you. Glancing at the symbol and consciously reminding yourself that it is okay to play can help resuscitate your levity.

It is up to us to defibrillate our funny bone. Only we have the means to get out our defibrillation paddles, turn on the juice, and then let 'er rip. We *can* GTXCITD.

❧

I love life.
I have a great sense of humor.
I love to laugh and get excited.

Carving Our Own Niche

WOMEN HAVE COME A LONG WAY SINCE A.D. 1500, when Spanish women were allowed to leave the house only three times: for their baptism as infants, to move into their husband's home, and to be buried.

Attitudes have changed a great deal since those repressive times, and men and women alike are now involved in a gentle (and, sometimes, not so gentle) revolution toward realness. We are working on finding our individual freedom by searching out what is right for each of us, free of stereotypes.

If we're to feel we are living our own life, not someone else's, it is imperative that we honor our unique calling. Dr. Elisabeth Kübler-Ross, the expert on death and dying, wisely noted, "The saddest people I see die are people who thought they could buy love by doing what mom and dad told them to do. They never listened to their own dreams. And they look back and say, 'I made a good living, but I never lived.' "

As she was growing up, Maureen loved playing with tools that were designated "boys' toys" by her parents. She liked building things; hammering and nailing boards together was a thrill. Her parents were horrified and, because she wanted and needed their approval, she abandoned her desire to build things. When she grew up, although it was not where her heart lay, Maureen became a secretary, a job looked upon as suitable by her parents. She was miserable.

Fortunately, Maureen awoke to the fact that she deserved to carve her own niche and, with the help of a therapist who assisted her in finding ways to communicate her true desires firmly but lovingly to her parents, became a carpenter.

In order to be our most creative selves, we need to accept the responsibility of carving out our own niche—searching for and seizing the activities and situations that are best suited to our unique abilities and aspirations.

I have a right to live my life.

I allow other people to be their own unique selves.

I give myself permission to follow my heart.

Colorizing Black and White

THERE ARE MANY OLD-MOVIE FANS, myself included, who lament the colorization of black-and-white films. It dilutes their charm. However, there is nothing charming about running old black-and-white movies in our minds, in the form of absolutes and inflexibilities, or archaic opinions about ourselves. We need to colorize those, to bring in shades, shadows, and perhaps some pastels, for there are exceptionally few pure whites and true blacks in real life.

Seeing issues only in black and white tends to rigidify our attitudes and beliefs. In order to develop our potential, we need to remain flexible and willing to change. Colorizing interior movies helps us gain perspective on our problems and discern whether our underlying assumptions are in need of updating. Since it's often true that we don't see things as they are, but as we are, it's important for our emotional, mental, and spiritual unfolding that we be able to see with technicolor eyes.

Shirley was tearfully telling me how conflicted she was about the decision she and her husband had made about moving to a smaller house. She oscillated between being okay and being sad and enraged. I asked her what made her unhappy, and she was surprised to realize that she was running an old movie in her mind of a sacrificing victim who never got what she wanted.

With further probing, Shirley realized that she had healed enough to never return to her old pattern of totally giving herself away, but the old black-and-white movie was still cranking away. She colorized it by remembering, and giving herself credit for, the new self-supporting behaviors she is now consistently doing.

Allowing ourselves to move from seeing only black and white into being able to distinguish shades of gray means it's only a matter of time, desire, and commitment before we can add bright colors to previously stark perspectives.

I see my life in bright and beautiful technicolor.

I let go of useless and restrictive beliefs and attitudes.

Observing and Elevating Thoughts

BECAUSE WE ARE SENTENCED TO THE consequences of our accumulated thoughts, it is important that we learn to observe and elevate them. Since thoughts are energy, they draw to them the same stuff they are made of. Therefore, if our thoughts are tin, what we draw to us will feel tinny and uncomfortable—sort of like chewing on aluminum foil.

All of us have nasty thoughts—critical, ugly, hateful, vengeful, intolerant, prejudiced—for we are human. And by observing and elevating our thoughts I'm not suggesting that we repress or sugarcoat our negative ones. If we do that, we empower them by pushing them into the deep recesses of our subconscious mind where they only grow stronger. I am suggesting that we not get *attached* to shadowy thoughts, but, rather, notice them and let them go. Being horrified and shamed by our negative thoughts can indelibly tatoo them on our psyches, whereas nonjudgmentally observing them for a moment allows thoughts to flow through and out of our minds.

For instance, I recently had the flu, and each

time I caught myself dwelling on how lousy I felt, I tried to remember to replace that thought in a couple of different ways. First, I gave thanks for the incredible healing machine that my body is, and affirmed that this, too, shall pass. Second, I visualized my body using this illness as an opportunity to cleanse and release all the toxins that had accumulated over the preceding year. Although elevating my thoughts to a plain higher than my physical discomfort did not cure the illness, it did improve my attitude and keep my optimism intact.

As an exercise in helping you observe and elevate your thoughts, imagine that everyone can read your mind. When a negative thought comes into your mind that you would rather keep to yourself, acknowledge it nonjudgmentally and then replace it with an uplifting one. Moving our thoughts to higher ground supports change in our lives.

I encourage negative thoughts to move rapidly through me.

My thoughts align with the purpose of my higher self.

Kicking the Worry Habit

WORRY IS A HABIT THAT KNOCKS THE supports right out from under us. So one of the most freeing changes we can make in our lives is to kick the worry habit. Since most habits are learned, it's important for us to ask where we learned to worry.

Rosa was a chronic worrier who came to see me in the hope that she could find relief from depression and insomnia. She said, "I was raised on worry and secondhand smoke, and I inhaled and absorbed the worry every bit as much as I did the smoke."

We explored the often unspoken but nevertheless powerful beliefs Rosa's parents had bequeathed. The majority of them were based on the assumptions that life was difficult, money was hard to come by, and God was a stern and punishing father. Rosa learned to believe that it never rained but it poured, there was never enough to go around, and that guilt was the only thing that could convince a vengeful God not to condemn her. Is it any wonder Rosa became a worrier?

The only lasting antidote for chronic worry is faith, faith in the good, faith that the Universal Mystery is for us rather than against us. If we have learned to believe in the unfortunate and hateful, we have the ability to change that and come to believe in goodness and love. I know it's possible because Rosa did it, and so did I. As Rosa was starting to change her belief system, I gave her a little card that read, *Sometimes we have many reasons to be unhappy and not many reasons to be happy. Our task is to be unreasonably happy.*

If you are plagued by the worry habit, simply becoming aware of worry when it overtakes you and deciding to affirm that life is good will set your feet firmly on the road to kicking the worry habit.

What we believe is our choice and we can support ourselves by choosing to be faith-filled and happy—even unreasonably so.

❦

I am safe.

God, the ultimate Mystery, loves and supports me.

I believe that life is good.

Taming the Coyote
in the Henhouse

OUR DAYS CAN BE FILLED WITH SUCH frenetic activity that peace of mind is lost and we feel as though we have stepped on a treadmill that is going way too fast. For our own well-being, we need to find ways to calm ourselves and slow down.

After hosting a wonderfully exuberant weekend party, I was so keyed up that I couldn't work or sleep. I felt like a coyote was in the henhouse of my mind and all the chickens were squawking and flapping madly in a cloud of feathers.

Needing to settle my feathers, I took a long, brisk walk to dissipate excess physical energy and then called a loving friend to share how scattered I felt. Only after exercise and expressing my feelings was I able to center myself through meditation. I created a peaceful atmosphere—candles, silence, and a view of nature—and sat down to meditate.

What is peaceful and conducive to contemplation for you? How often do you allow yourself the luxury (or, it could be argued, the *necessity*) of uninterrupted tranquil time? If you don't often experience rejuvenating solitude in which serenity can blossom, now is the time to give yourself the boon of allowing that.

After establishing a setting that is soothing to you, rest in it. Give yourself permission to simply *be* in the place you have made. There are no rules. Just be you. After several minutes of quiet, visualize your mind's activity. You may want to use my coyote/henhouse analogy or anything else that seems appropriate to you. Consciously encourage your mind to rest. Gently, slowly, as though watching a storm abate, create a calmer atmosphere. If the whirlwind persists, tenderly assure your mind that it's okay to be quiet and allow it to respond positively to that suggestion.

Although it isn't easy to do in our scattered and scattering environment, we have the power to tame the coyote in the henhouse and create mental and emotional harmony out of pandemonium.

I am calm and peaceful.
Serenity is possible even in the midst of chaos.

Using Our Rage

HARNESSING THE FORCE OF OUR RAGE as we harness and dam flowing water in order to create electricity is a powerful way for women to institute needed changes in society. I believe rage is different than anger in that it touches feelings more intense than anger and is more universal. It is a mighty force that can be used for our benefit when channeled constructively. Rage is the consequence of cumulative disrespect and devaluation. Anger fumes for *us*, whereas rage flares for the *whole*.

Rachel was involved in a fender bender and felt mildly irritated with the other driver, who was at fault, because of the inconvenience the accident would create for her. However, when he jokingly made a remark to the policeman about women drivers, she was instantly catapulted into rage. What in her had been triggered by that remark? Perhaps a profound resentment at the casual put-downs women endure or maybe an intense rebellion against the feminine being devalued by the masculine. Whatever the reason, a core issue of Rachel's was ignited and rage was the result. Luckily for the rest of us women, she did not keep silent about her feelings, and the outcome of her speaking up was an apology from the other driver.

Virginia Woolf's statement, "Scratch a woman and you'll find a rage" is indicative of our unwillingness to allow injustice to reign. Rage is the fuel of revolution. We women, with fires burning deeply in our hearts over the ills in our world, country, community, and in our own homes, have the ability to be a revolutionary force to be reckoned with as we fight for love, personal freedom, and an awareness of the connectedness of all persons and things.

Instead of dousing the flames of our rage, let us, with deep commitment, fan the embers and coolly, calmly, lovingly dam and direct our rage for the good of ourselves, others, and Mother Earth. May the conscious flow of our collective rage light the path for new supportive attitudes and irrigate our collective conscience with ideas of equality for *all*.

*I have the courage to speak up
when faced with injustice.*

*I have the wisdom and the right to use
my rage constructively.*

Keeping Relationships Current

RECENTLY ONE OF MY DEAREST FRIENDS gave me a verbal bouquet of roses. We were saying goodbye after a lengthy, heart-filling long-distance conversation when I said, "Words can't describe how much I love you, you know!" and she answered, "No, but your behavior does, on a consistent basis."

I was struck by how incredibly true her statement was about all relationships. Does our behavior match our commitment to another? Do we keep valued relationships current through attention and caring or do we get caught up in the whirlpool of busyness and ignore people we love?

Relationships are as important to us women as the very air we breathe. Without relationships we feel bereft, cut off from vital sources of comfort and support. Yet, with our busy schedules, have we been able to make it a priority to keep our relationships current? Luckily, most of our heart-held relationships, those that add to our lives and multiply our blessings, are fairly drought-resistant and can thrive on bursts of concentrated love and attention. But if nurturing and sustaining our relationships feels like yet another energy-draining obligation, we need to change our perception and see friendship as a sacred, life-enhancing gift we give and receive.

Elizabeth Yates wrote a beautiful passage in her book *Up the Golden Stair,* "Keep your relationships current. Follow the impulse to do that small kindness for another whenever it comes to you. Then you will never be beset by the thought, Oh, if I had only done it when I thought of it—This is one of the discoveries I have made this year: that if the inner promptings of heart and mind are obeyed there will never be an echo of the words 'too late.'"

Open your heart for a moment and allow your intuition to clue you in to who needs a supportive word from you today. What kindness, compliment, or moment of your time can you give to someone with whom you want to keep your relationship current?

❦

I nurture and sustain my relationships through following my urges to give.

I am a trustworthy friend to myself and others.

Inviting Abundance

Life begets life. Energy creates energy.
It is by spending oneself that one becomes
rich.

—*Sarah Bernhardt*

A FRIEND OF MINE ATTENDING A conference was surprised to notice that everyone at the breakfast table had coffee but her. She felt a little miffed and said, "Why didn't I get coffee?" Someone answered, "You have to turn your cup over, June, in order for them to pour you some." Ah, isn't that what we often do, forget to turn our cup up to receive?

Why do we often have such qualms about anticipating and accepting abundance? Maybe it's because historically we women rendered services that were largely taken for granted—rather than respected and reimbursed—and we learned to give to others but not expect anything for ourselves. In order to invite abundance into our lives we need to feel worthy of the myriad blessings life has to offer: supportive relationships, peace of mind, well-balanced kids, health, enough money, and satisfying work to name a few.

Whatever the reasons for our hesitancy in accepting all forms of prosperity into our lives, it is important *now* that we change any limiting beliefs and awake to the realization that we deserve to live abundant lives both practically and emotionally.

Flowing with the Current

HAVE YOU EVER GONE ON A RIVER-rafting trip? If you have, imagine what it would have been like if your guide thought it would be interesting to have you go *up* the river rather than down. The excitement of the trip would wane very quickly as you attempted the arduous task of fighting the current by going against the flow.

We wouldn't accept a guide like that, would we? But in our inner lives, so often we do just that! Daily our attitudes and beliefs about abundance launch us into the river of life and cause us to struggle upstream. If, for instance, we think that life is like a pie and there's not enough to go around, we will end up hungry. Or, if we believe that we deserve only a meager supply of respect, happiness, or dollars, that's probably what we will receive—which feels a lot like bucking the current.

Years ago, while taking a workshop on prosperity, a woman friend and I came face-to-face with limiting beliefs that kept us from entering the flow of abundance. We were asked to write down how much yearly income we wanted. While most of the men in the group blithely threw around figures with lots of zeros, Bonnie and I both came up with very conservative numbers. We worried about what others would think, wondered if we were deserving, and feared we wouldn't be loved and accepted if we had generous incomes.

We women need to uproot old self-denying beliefs about money and view prosperity as freedom—freedom to do more for ourselves and to be of better service to others. We need to encourage each other in learning to value our talent by accepting, as worthy, our ability to earn money.

When we believe that we are worthy to receive and that the universe benevolently wishes to give to us, we can flow *with* the stream of abundance and feel well cared for and wealthy no matter what the circumstances. Abundance is, in large part, an attitude.

❦

I deserve to live abundantly.

*Life is an abundant blessing and
I am worthy of every smidgen.*

Setting Our Sails

ONE OF THE MOST SUPPORTIVE THINGS
we can learn to do for ourselves is to open up to
receiving what we want, need, and deserve. So
often we know we need to receive, but we don't
know how. We're very good at giving, but
sometimes grapple blindly with the ability to
take. We move through our lives like a sailboat
with its sails tightly furled. The good news is
that even the most entrenched givers among us
can invite abundance into our lives by discovering how to set our sails so that the wind can
catch and fill them. But first we must know that
it is okay for us to get as well as to give.

Toward that end, sit comfortably with your
back straight and begin to focus your attention
away from the activities of the day and toward
an awareness of the present moment only. If
your mind wanders, gently bring it back to the
here and now. If your body feels uncomfortable,
rearrange it in a better position. Quietly begin
to think of water—relaxing, soothing water.
Allow the image of a lake, ruffled by a gentle
breeze, to come into your mind's eye. Seeing
that you are in a marina filled with sailboats,
you intuitively realize that you know how to

sail. Choose the boat that most appeals to you and launch her into the lake.

Now become aware of what you want to do. Float? Row? If you prefer to sail, with great expertise and effortlessness visualize yourself unfurling the sails and setting them in the perfect way. Lean back on your cushions with your hand on the tiller and allow the wind to work for you. How does it feel to easily glide over the water, tacking to catch the optimum breezes? If it feels good, continue to enjoy the experience. If you are uncomfortable, gently allow yourself to move back to a place where you feel safe and secure and assure yourself that you deserve to receive all the good that you want.

Be gentle as you gain the confidence to accept from others as well as give to them. It's not easy to change, but through trust and self-support, we can come to really *know* that it is okay for us to open our sails.

I am able to receive easily and graciously.

*Love and light flow to and from me
in ever-increasing amounts.*

Aging Successfully

WE OFTEN DREAD AGING, BUT IT CAN actually bring with it our greatest sense of comfort and security. Author Jean Shinoda Bolen researched the times in women's lives when they felt the happiest. Her results were surprising: the happiest women were often those who lived alone and were between the ages of sixty and seventy. These women obviously knew how to age successfully.

It is possible for us to learn to enjoy aging by concentrating on the gains inherent in it rather than the losses. To help me focus on the positives as I age, I adopt a new motto each decade. In this decade, my credo is *Fifty is Freedom*. My fifties have brought me the freedom of no longer being chained to "What will *they* think?" but instead, "What do *I* think?" What a blessing and a relief! A wonderful compensation for swaying underarms.

To help you focus on the abundant advantages of aging, jot down some of the joys and freedoms you've gained from living as many years as you have. What lessons have you learned? What emotional chains have you loosened? What wounds have you healed? Take a moment to give thanks for these benefits of aging.

Calmly close your eyes and visualize yourself as a wise and peaceful old woman. See the woman you are today bestowing upon that venerable older you the respect she so richly deserves. Ask her what she wants and needs from you today to ensure that she will continue to age successfully. Are you willing to give her what she requests? If not, ask yourself why. What are you afraid of? If you can give your aged self what she needs, assure her of your willingness to do so and ask if she has any wisdom she would like to give you now. When you feel complete with this meeting, tenderly leave her, knowing that you can return to her side whenever you desire.

Gratitude for the abundance of experiences and wisdom we have accumulated through the years helps us to age successfully.

❧

Each year I grow in wisdom and acceptance.

I am comfortable with the age I am now.

Pigging Out on Life

AUNTIE MAME, THE QUEEN OF ABUNDANT living, tells her nephew, "Life is a banquet and some poor fools are starving to death!" in order to teach him to enjoy life to the fullest—to pig out on life Unfortunately, that's not the message many of us interpreted from what we observed growing up.

Many of us carry into adulthood the vague feeling that abundance is somehow bad. Perhaps those ideas were spawned while learning to share our toys as children, or were a misinterpretation of the oft-heard, "Money is the root of all evil." Even though the Bible verse condemns the *love* of money, not money itself, we feel guilty pigging out on prosperity and settle for gumming life into a numbing blandness.

Even less fortunate than those of us who assumed from society that it is better to be deprived than privileged are those who were told directly that *they*, personally, were unworthy of privileges. I commented to my client Vanessa on how pretty her bracelet was and to my surprise tears sprang to her eyes.

Vanessa, an incest victim, had worn the bracelet on a visit to her parents' home, and her mother said, "Why do you think you deserve to spend that much money on something as frivolous as that?" Needless to say, Vanessa was crushed and vowed that she would not wear the bracelet again until her wounded inner little girl was healed enough to understand her mother's warped attitude and strong enough not to take her put-downs so to heart. Vanessa's tears honored the pain she had endured as a child and the determination she had shown in moving beyond it. The bracelet had become her silver badge of courage.

To help us learn to pig out on life, we can adopt an inner Auntie Mame who unfailingly tells us that we're worthy of partaking of the banquet and no longer need to starve in the midst of plenty. As we begin to value ourselves as lovable, unique beings who have the right to live life to the fullest, we will grow in our ability to accept all the good available to us and believe that, as Julia Child says, "Life is the proper binge."

❦

I am a unique and lovable woman.

I am free to pig out joyously when appropriate.

I choose to live!

Kissing the Hand
That Feeds Us

TO FEEL AS THOUGH WE ARE LIVING abundantly, the first thing to do is fall in love with ourselves—to kiss the hand that feeds us instead of snapping and snarling at it. I know that may sound narcissistic but it really isn't. Appreciating ourselves teaches others to treat us better and means that the person we are always with—ourself—is in our corner.

An experience I had at a restaurant gave me an amusing framework for the idea of kissing the hand that feeds us. The handsome and suave waiter graciously, and it seemed sincerely, referred to me as "Beautiful Lady" throughout the meal. He caringly laid the napkin in my lap, leapt to fill my water glass, and even rushed outside to tell me goodnight as I left. He *served* me during that all-too-short meal, and I felt cherished as the object of his chivalrous attention. His was the most generous tip I've ever given, and it was well worth it.

Later, as I was chuckling over the feelings I had during that dinner, I thought, What if we graciously and caringly waited on ourselves?

What if we served ourselves in ways that made us feel special? What if we were solicitously aware of our needs and enthusiastically hastened to fill them? If we treated ourselves this well, might we not return that favorable treatment with liberal gratuities of increased confidence and an abiding sense of self-worth?

Give yourself the gift of a day in which you wait on yourself as my waiter did me. This does not mean that you necessarily change your routine, but for this one day—which, hopefully, will stretch into a lifetime—make it your joy and privilege to ask yourself, "What can I get you to make this day better? How may I serve you right now?" Learning to kiss the hand that feeds us means that it will gladly pat our cheek in return.

❧

*I am a beautiful, unique being and
treat myself accordingly.*

*I joyfully fill my own needs and have the courage
to ask for what I want and need from others.*

Stoking the Fires of Creativity

ELIZABETH BARRETT BROWNING ONCE said, "Light tomorrow with today!" Great advice, and following it means we have to get fired up *today*, aflame with the desire to follow our dreams.

To fan the flames, we need to be enthusiastically supportive of our ideas, no matter how crazy or farfetched they seem. We are *all* creative—we have only to tune in to our night dreams to verify that—but so many of us throw the cold water of "I can't do that" or "My ideas aren't *really* very good" onto our original notions. Dampened by doubt, the fires of creativity can fizzle. It's up to us to fan the flames of our own creativity. Believing in ourselves is the most powerful bellows we can use to kindle the fire of creative thought.

Another good way to help a tiny creative ember become a raging fire is to make it *fun!* Gather people around you who help you keep your ideas aflame by treating them respectfully, but *lightly*. When we take ourselves too seriously we dry up. But if we enjoy the process and excitedly brainstorm about our ideas, the creative juices flow.

In order to begin oiling your creative cogs, quickly, without really thinking, jot down at least six completions to this statement: If I believed in myself, I would _____.
Just as quickly and nonjudgmentally finish this sentence: If I gave myself permission to follow my dreams, I would _____.
Play with what your sentences tell you. Make up some of your own sentence starts and then finish them. Catch fire and play with the process.

You are creative! Dare to do new things. Stretch and risk. It is okay to try and fail. In fact, when we're truly creative, failure is an essential part of the process. The only true failure is not trying. We can tap into abundant creativity by believing in ourselves and getting fired up.

❦

I believe in my own creativity.

I enjoy trying new things and having new ideas.

I lighten up and play with my creative thoughts.

Becoming a Conduit of Grace

THERE ARE PEOPLE WHO SEEM TO BE lightning rods for grace. From them flows an almost visible vibration of compassion, and to be around them is to feel blessed and uplifted. Some are saints and some are *ordinary* people who have the extraordinary ability to allow respect and kindness to flow through them—not all the time, but at least on occasion.

Several years ago I had the opportunity to watch someone become such a conduit. I was with Dr. Elisabeth Kübler-Ross when she went to see a patient. As we walked toward the young woman's room, Elisabeth was grousing about something and I remember thinking she was in an irritable mood.

Although an irritated doctor pushed open the door, a radiant, grace-filled, and compassionate woman walked into the room. I could only watch in awe as love emanated from Elisabeth to the beautiful quadriplegic lying on the bed. In the space of the few minutes we stayed, that hospital room was converted from a sad and impersonal last stop to a sanctuary of acceptance and peace.

I think that one of the reasons Elisabeth is such a wonderful conduit of grace is that she is totally committed to bringing peace and comfort to the dying and bereaved. Because her *intention* is absolutely clear, even in the midst of irritation, she can move into a centered place and allow healing energy to flow through her. If Elisabeth can do it, so can we.

Close your eyes and gently focus on your breathing, allowing it to move in and out naturally. For a few minutes think of nothing but your breath. Without effort, bring your mind back to your breath as it wanders off. Ask yourself what type of grace you would like to become the conduit for today. Visualize yourself walking through your day as though you already *were* such a conduit. How does it feel? Notice how your grace-giving affects the people you meet. Allow that grace to flow to you, through you to others, and return to you.

We can become a loving conduit for the grace that fits our particular journey.

I am a conduit of grace.
Loves flows to me and through me.

Flying with a Tailwind

ABUNDANCE COULD BE DESCRIBED AS the knack of living in an attitude of gratitude. If we constantly run on fast forward, frantically trying to keep up with what *should* and *must* be done, without taking a break to restore ourselves and count our blessings, we'll soon run out of gas. Stopping for a rest, pausing to really see the wonder in our world, and making room for interludes of thankfulness helps give us the energy to keep going.

Gratitude is a tailwind that enables us to travel farther and faster. An elderly relative of my husband's is almost an invalid and yet has a joyous spirit. Many of her conversations begin with such statements as, "Isn't it wonderful that...?" "Have you ever seen a more beautiful day?" and "I am so lucky to have such wonderful friends!" Of course she has her low times, but with the resilience of a superball, she bounces back into an attitude of gratitude.

The flip side of that optimism was the attitude of a woman I spoke with who has been a hospice volunteer for several years. I was astounded when she said, "I don't see *anything* good in *any* of this illness stuff." None of us is in love with disease and death, but how sad for this woman, *and* the families she was sent to serve, that she never found the roses among the thorns.

Give yourself the priceless gift of extricating yourself from the whirlwind for a few minutes and write down all the things, just within sight, for which you feel grateful. Expand your list to include people and circumstances out of sight. As a bonus, add to your list some intangibles—attitudes, experiences, philosophies, etc. Looking at your list, allow your heart to open in a flow of gratitude and appreciation. Visualize that flow of thankfulness enveloping you like an iridescent mist that reaches out to embrace all those with whom you come in contact.

Flying with a tailwind of gratitude helps us savor the effortless times and move more quickly through the turbulent times.

I am grateful for my life.

I am especially grateful for _____.

I appreciate life, both the chaff and the grain.

Soaring from the Empty Nest

CONTRARY TO THE POPULAR OLD WIVES' TALE (old mothers' tale might be more apropos here), women are not always bereft at the emptying of the nest. Many, in fact, find it one of the most liberating and abundant times of life.

Of course there are exceptions. Women who have no interests of their own outside the family or have used their children as their only emotional support, or those of us who have never learned to think of our own needs without guilt, may well fall prey to depression as the children leave. Since we can look forward to about thirty post-children years, it's important we start now to ensure that those decades will be meaningful and fun.

If your children are still at home, sit quietly in a place where you will not be disturbed (the bathroom was sometimes my last bastion of privacy) and picture yourself as a mid-life woman in an adult-only household. If you feel anticipation and excitement, you're probably one of those who will easily soar from the empty nest. If the thought of no children at home is troublesome, ask yourself where you are stuck in the mothering process. What do you need to do in order to release your kids into their adulthood and yourself into your fertile mid-years and beyond?

If you are already an "empty-nester" and are enjoying yourself, know that you are in good company. But, if your life feels barren with daily mothering behind you, honor your individual existence by courageously opening the next door. Bring your personal dreams out of the closet and dust them off. Look at your situation in terms of the freedoms you have gained—jot them down—instead of the loss of role and rights. Remember who you were *before* having children and explore who you want to be *now*. If you feel bogged down, seek help, for it is possible to revel in this time of life, gleaning wisdom and giving joy.

I carefully create a life of my own and
allow my children to do the same.

Wheeeeeee! I'm free to be me!

Growing through Loss

I like living. I have sometimes been wildly, despairingly, acutely miserable, racked with sorrow, but through it all I still know quite certainly that just to be alive is a grand thing.

—*Agatha Christie*

LOSS IN LIFE IS UNAVOIDABLE, and descending into the grief of loss is, initially, a plunge into emotional hell. When racked with raw sorrow we simply need to survive, finding what comfort and solace we can from sources that nurture and sustain us. Fresh pain requires sustaining support—shoulders upon which to lean and cry. In order to heal naturally, and grow through our pain, we must first allow ourselves to feel it.

In spite of the pain, grief can also be the doorway to the rich cavern of our being, the sanctuary of our soul. Growing through loss enables us to evolve into deeper levels of confidence and maturity. When we are committed to growth, we will, step by tiny step, make the arduous climb out of the pit of loss carrying the precious jewels of strength, resilience, and a greater capacity for empathy and caring.

For those of us who, in our grief, consciously move toward a deeper acceptance and understanding of ourselves and God, the abyss of despair can become an incubator for compassion and spiritual conviction. If we are to remain emotionally healthy, we can't avoid the excruciating kiln of grief, but out of the searing fire can come a more beautiful and service-full vessel.

Allowing the Grieving Process

GRIEF IS A PROCESS. ONLY WHEN IT IS allowed to unfold naturally can profound healing take place. There are several stages of grief that most people move in to and out of during the process of recovering from loss. They are fear and panic, shock and denial, anger, bargaining, depression, and, finally, acceptance. They are listed roughly in the order many people experience them, but since emotions are rarely neat and tidy, it is perfectly natural to skip some stages or shift back and forth between others.

The old adage "Ignore it and maybe it'll go away" might be true of some things, but not grief. Ignore grief, and it will stay, gnawing at our innards. Therefore, in order to fully heal, we need to acknowledge and trust the grieving process and muster the courage to go through it by seeking solace and support along the way.

Because grief is so intense, while in the midst of it you may feel as though you have gone crazy. In order to reassure yourself of your sanity, I strongly suggest joining a bereavement support group. Being able to talk honestly with others who are experiencing similar emotions is extremely freeing and healing. There are also many wonderful books available that describe the stages of grief in detail. Reading them can be very helpful, but please don't get discouraged if you find it impossible to concentrate on them at first. Lack of concentration is a scary but natural and temporary part of the grieving process.

The ultimate goal of the grieving process is acceptance of our loss and commitment to creating a new, fulfilling life within the altered circumstances. Healthy acceptance does not mean martyred resignation or fatalism, but rather a serene understanding that resisting circumstances over which we have no control only causes us more pain. As a result of allowing ourselves to grieve naturally, burning out anguish by accepting and honestly acknowledging our feelings, peace of mind will return.

I have the courage to grieve.

I care for and nurture myself, especially when experiencing pain.

I reach out to others when I need support.

Cradling a Staggering Heart

OUR HEARTS CAN STAGGER UNDER THE weight of many hurts. Whether the injury is large or small, being cradled by support and nurtured by kindness is essential as we stumble through the pain back to equilibrium.

Having a tender and accepting attitude toward ourselves while racked with pain provides much needed inner comfort, but it is imperative that we allow outside support also. In not-so-rare incidences, inner and outer support can combine in miraculous ways. One early morning after the death of my mother, I was driving speedily down the freeway when I heard a strange noise and felt the urge to pull off onto the shoulder of the road. As I slowed from seventy-something to a crawl, my tire exploded—no piece larger than a handkerchief remained. Surveying the damage, I gave thanks for my safety and said aloud, "Mother, was that *you* warning me?"

The response was my own involuntary burst of tears and an inner awareness of the words, You are my child, I will take care of you. My heart, staggering from the loss of not only a mother but a cherished friend, was cradled by her continuing concern.

As an exercise in cradling yourself with comfort, close your eyes and place your hands over your heart. For a few quiet moments, concentrate on the rhythm of your heart. Give thanks for its faithfulness. Allow to come into your mind's eye a picture of yourself when in pain. With your hands still protecting your heart, compassionately observe the you who is hurting. Who is she? What does she look like? What is she feeling? Who is there, in your inner family, who can comfort her? What person or thing outside of her can cradle her as she grieves? Visualize her being comforted in whatever way your wise subconscious presents. Soak in the nurturing, and permit your heart to open and receive compassion and eventual healing.

In the advent of pain, cradle your staggering heart as willingly as you would a precious infant.

❧

I am as willing to cradle my own heart as I am to cradle others'.

I allow others to nurture and support me.

Moving toward
Balance and Harmony

LIFE IS AN UNCEASING CYCLE OF BIRTH, death, and rebirth. Revolving changes, losses and gains. Our often difficult lesson is learning to remain balanced and in harmony with ourselves no matter what the circumstances.

In attempting to come to grips with our fluctuating fortunes, we can look to Mother Nature for inspiration. In her is a flowing balance of opposites—moving toward and retreating from, warmth and cold, light and darkness, summer and winter. Mother Nature teaches us that there is a season for all happenings. She gives us hope, while in the core of darkness, that *this*, too, *shall* pass.

I received a letter from a young widow who is a beautiful example of a woman who, through adversity, has learned to achieve balance and harmony within. Jo Ann was just forty-one when her husband died from a brain tumor. She was left to raise five children, the youngest of whom has Down's syndrome. As if that weren't enough, her husband had let his life insurance lapse, and she was stranded with no money to live on, let alone pay the astronomical medical bills that had accumulated.

The past several years have been ones of triumphs and tragedy for Jo Ann and her children, but her letter was upbeat. It said, in part, "I'm enjoying my newfound freedom, my sense of direction, and, of course, my five great kids." Tacked to the letter was a cartoon, captioned, "Illness is healing."

Out of the crucible of death and despair, Jo Ann forged a new life by supporting herself emotionally and asking for the encouragement and comfort she needed.

In order to feel more harmonious, do yourself a freeing favor and make a list of ways in which you need to support yourself *today*. Jot down what you want and the areas in which you need to say no. Maybe more of *you* needs to be put on the scales of your life in order for them to balance properly.

❦

I accept and incorporate change in my life.

I help balance and harmonize my life
by not forgetting myself.

I believe that this, too, shall pass.

Inspecting the Tide Pools

THE DUCHESS OF WINDSOR ONCE WROTE, "A woman's life can really be a succession of lives, each revolving around some emotionally compelling situation or challenge, and each marked off by some intense experience." As the duchess suggests, our lives and feelings have a natural ebb and flow; we exist in a continuum of tranquil and turbulent seas. One of our main assignments as self-aware beings is to explore both our high and low tides.

It is easy to accept the rhythm of life when we're riding the crest of its waves, exhilarated by its effortless flow. Far more difficult is accepting our low tides, the ebbs and storms life presents. In order to grow in understanding and awareness we must accept the challenge of exploring our inner tide pools exposed as the ocean recedes.

After we are hit with an emotional tsunami, it's very valuable to inspect the tide pools laid bare by the adversity. Here we can gather the information we need to create an emotionally self-supportive life. However, exposing our vulnerable, wounded areas can prove to be the easy part; working through them may be arduous and slow, but, ultimately, liberating. As we grow through the aftermath of loss, we often need the comforting arms of supportive friends and perhaps the guidance of an excellent therapist.

Gently explore your tide pools. What vulnerabilities are uncovered in your low times? What strengths? Ask yourself what you can do to support yourself emotionally during life's ebbs, and then commit to accepting yourself during both high and low tides.

There is a rich sea of knowledge and understanding to be explored when we encourage ourselves to inspect the wonders of our own inner tide pools. These discoveries can become the lifeboats in which we ride out the varying tides of our successive lives.

❧

I value the lessons learned in low times.

I am strong and capable.

I am a survivor and thriver.

Opening the Door to Pain

IN ORDER TO LOVINGLY SUPPORT ourselves, we must go *gently* into the dark nights of our soul, but go in we must. Just as we are taught to turn into the skid on an icy road in order to regain control of our car, we need to turn *into* our feelings rather than *away* from them. Only by turning into and then moving *through* our feelings can we gain control of them and emerge into the light of healing.

Never is it more important for us to take care of ourselves than when we are standing on the threshold of pain. We need to be protected by friends who can listen nonjudgmentally and support us unconditionally. But we must also be there for ourselves, cultivating an internal intimacy that is sympathetic, accepting, and trusting.

Opening the door to our pain means that we let ourselves feel it, examine it, and then release it—or at least have an intention to let it go. If we can meet our pain while securely centered in the sacred heart of the Divine, we will be less terrified and more willing to confront it.

As an experiment in finding a sacred center, sit quietly in a place in which you feel especially comfortable. Concentrate on bringing warmth and light to your heart. With your eyes closed, visualize a soft stream of shimmering light emanating from your heart. Just as you would a flashlight, direct your heart light toward a space about eight to ten feet from you. Very slowly and naturally imagine a loving Being beginning to form in the midst of your light. In the Being's presence you feel secure and safe, totally loved and accepted. As it beckons to you, move to the Being's side where you are enfolded in a sustaining embrace. Linger in the calming peace until you feel ready to gently open your eyes, understanding that this Being wants to be with you whenever you call.

❦

I am worthy of resting in the sacred heart
of the Divine.

I am a caring friend to myself.

I am supportive of myself and others when a painful door
needs opening.

Accepting Respite Care

TO BE TAKEN CARE OF WHILE IN PAIN IS a deep yearning shared by all of us, men and women alike. While thrashing around in confusion or anguish, how wonderfully healing it is to be held safely in supportive arms. Yet so often when we need care and support the most, we isolate ourselves from others. Why?

Several reasons come to mind: we don't want to be a burden; we are more comfortable being a care *giver* than a *receiver*; we feel we do not have the right to be *down*; or we are ashamed of our feelings and think we are being overemotional.

In order to regain our confidence and become gently strong, we need to learn to accept respite care—to allow ourselves to be nurtured and cared for when our strength has dwindled and we are low on reserves. When ill, we will heal more rapidly if we give others the invaluable gift of being able to minister to us. If the shock of grief renders us shaky, disoriented, and unable to sleep well, it's supremely important to recognize that now is the time to lean back into the protective embrace of those who love us and want to care for us. Stubbornly refusing help is counterproductive to the return of strength, whereas encouraging ourselves to temporarily lay down the burdens of responsibility creates a climate in which healing can take root.

We all have times when the emotional and physical pins are knocked out from under us. Even though it may go against our nature or feel foreign to us, sometimes the wisest and strongest thing we can do is admit our weakness and have the courage to accept extensive care from others.

I have the courage to admit my weaknesses.

I accept and welcome help from others when I am in need.

I find it natural to both give and receive.

Mourning Invites Morning

GRIEF IS A SLEEP ROBBER. THOSE LONG, black hours from approximately three A.M. to dawn can be the most devastating during grieving, an isolated walk through the valley of darkness. Being awake in Mother Nature's darkness forces us to face the darkness within ourselves. Finding constructive ways to mourn in those lonely hours, ways that invite the morning of the new day as well as a sunrise of healing within ourselves, is a tremendous challenge, but we do have the inner strength to accomplish it.

Anger and resistance may be bedfellows that keep us too agitated to sleep. We may want to avoid our emotions because we fear that allowing them would overwhelm us with such rage and sorrow that we would never again regain our equilibrium. If that is the case, it's better to get out of bed and *express* our feelings through writing them out or drawing a vivid picture, for instance, rather than lying there, becoming more upset and frustrated by the minute.

One sleepless night during my divorce I was so churned up by feelings of rage and betrayal that I called the Suicide Prevention crisis number. Luckily for me, the phone was answered by a very rude young man who didn't want his sleep interrupted by someone who was not bleeding to death or had not swallowed a lethal amount of something or other. His callous reaction to me was the perfect excuse to vent my anger with men. I will give him credit for staying on the line as I lambasted men in general, and him and my husband in particular. That call provided a safe place for me, a dedicated "nice girl," to dispose of some accumulated grief and venom. Afterward, I slept, and morning arrived as scheduled.

Grief does feel overwhelming at times, but it's more likely to overpower us when we shun it than it is when we courageously feel it. Avoiding the feelings released so relentlessly during the night only generates suppression, not healing.

I have the courage to feel my feelings.

I express my grief constructively.

*I am strong and able to transcend and
heal my wounds.*

Defrosting a Frozen Heart

SOMETIMES, WHEN TOO MUCH PAIN assails us at once, we protect ourselves by going into emotional deep freeze. Perhaps that works to insulate us from the depth of our pain, but it also blocks intimacy with ourselves and others by numbing our ability to reach out and respond. Protecting ourselves via a frozen heart suspends us in a hardened state of apathy and lethargy.

Knowing that we only ice up when we feel a tremendous compulsion to insulate ourselves from our wounds alerts us to our need to defrost slowly, patiently, and with great care. Never should we strip away our protection too rapidly, for if we do, we run the risk of exposing raw and defenseless parts of ourselves before they are ready. Please do yourself the service of seeking help during the first stages of "defrosting."

One of the most common ways we attempt to protect ourselves is by breathing as shallowly as possible. Therefore, a gentle and effective way to begin the defrosting process is to consciously breathe deeply into the pain rather than away from it.

As soon as I saw Brenda enter the restaurant, I knew something was wrong. When I asked her, she answered, "Nothing! I can't talk about it." I took her hand and simply said, "Breathe, Brenda, breathe." She did, and out poured a torrent of cleansing tears. By letting herself breathe through her armor, Brenda truly felt the pain she was experiencing, and healing could begin.

Softly sit in a quiet place (a public restaurant will probably not be your choice) and calmly direct your attention to your body. Notice if there are areas that feel tight or tense. Breathe deeply into those places, asking your breath to gently dislodge any stored feelings needing attention. If feelings come up, observe them and let them pass, or easily open your eyes and write down what you are experiencing—do what feels right to you. Continue breathing gently and deeply. Experience the flood of warmth as your body opens. We have the power to dissolve that protection when we choose.

❧

I trust myself.

I am safe.

I am gentle and kind to myself.

Finding Solace
in the Everlasting Arms

WE ARE IN NEED OF COMFORT REGULARLY, but never so acutely as when we are experiencing loss. It doesn't matter what form it takes, as shattering as death or divorce or as simple as a thoughtless remark. Whatever the loss, the vulnerable part of us yearns for comfort and support that can come from many sources—friends, family, self-acceptance, pets, uplifting reading, and spiritual beliefs.

As a little girl, Shoshana loved the Bible verse about the everlasting arms of God being underneath us all. She pictured God as the traditional white-robed, bearded grandfather and often felt herself carried securely in His arms. Her childlike trust in a loving Father began to evaporate as the "realities" of life imposed themselves upon her; eventually she became a practicing apathetic, not thinking much about the Mystery that she had trusted implicitly as a child.

Shoshana's adult life became strewn with obstacles. She told me that one night, feeling bereft, she sank to the floor, too emotionally spent to say anything except, "Help me. Please, help me." Suddenly the room filled with a luminous presence and, from its brilliance, two larger-than-life arms draped in diaphanous gold material lifted her into their compassionate embrace. Resonating in her head was the message, *Underneath are the everlasting arms.*

I would like you to sit quietly, maybe in candlelight, and allow your breath to deepen. With each inhalation, imagine that you are breathing in acceptance. As you exhale invite yourself to release any mistrust or self-condemnation you may have accumulated. Visualize the inhaled acceptance gently soothing and bringing solace to your heart. Warmed by the tender touch of acceptance, feel your heart begin to open and heal. Bask in the loving climate of approval you are permitting to surround you.

When we have fallen against a jagged place in the road, it is wise, not weak, to seek solace, trusting our hearts to the Divine Mystery whose arms are forever waiting to guide and console.

❦

God is in every breath I take.

Underneath are the everlasting arms.

Wishing at the Well

TO LOVE IS TO RISK LOSS, BUT NOT TO love is to ensure emotional death. Therefore, if we choose to really *live*, we will need to accept a certain amount of grief as well. None of us says, "Oh goody, another opportunity to grow!" when confronted with loss and pain; in fact, our basic wish is to avoid plunging into the well of grief. But sometimes we have no choice. And if we don't avail ourselves of emotional support at those difficult times, we run the risk of closing our hearts in order to escape sorrow.

When Glenna's young husband died, she felt as though her life had ended also. For many months she was so paralyzed with grief that she found it almost impossible to clean her house, let alone leave it. She walled herself away from everyone, both physically and emotionally. Exhausted from a sleepless, tearful night, she "saw" herself crouched in the fetal position enclosed in a huge glass bell jar. She felt isolated in the jar, but protected—no one could reach her to hurt her; but she was also imprisoned within it and unable to reach out to anyone.

Luckily for Glenna, a few of her friends continued to tap on her bell jar until she finally agreed to see a therapist. With her help, Glenna discovered that her fear of accepting her husband's death was grounded in a primal belief that she would actually die from the pain. Because of this anxiety, isolating herself felt like the only way to survive. Gently Glenna's therapist guided her to trust that there was more to her than her pain. As she began to accept herself as strong and capable of withstanding her grief, Glenna was able to release herself from the prison of her emotional quarantine. She began to support herself as well as reach out to others. As she trusted that she could heal, healing began.

Within each of us is a wellspring of healing powers. Our task is to be confident that we are equal to our challenges and accept ourselves as powerfully resilient even while feeling frail and vulnerable.

I have a wellspring of healing within me.

I am a survivor.

I can do all things through God who strengthens me.

Re-potting Ourselves

LOSS CHANGES OUR ENVIRONMENT and, therefore, changes *us*. It is essential that we adapt to our new conditions, re-potting ourselves, fertilizing and feeding the shaken bloom that we are after a traumatic change, so that our roots can reach into a greater faith and trust in ourselves and our ability to survive and thrive.

After the sudden death of her only child, Cathy said that she felt like a plant ripped out of the ground by an angry, malevolent beast who continued to violently shake her while her naked roots whipped about helplessly. The death of a child is one of the most excruciating losses anyone can sustain, and the re-potting process after such a blow can be painfully slow but is possible. Cathy is a good example of positive re-potting. She began the profound task of surviving her loss by seeking therapy immediately after her son's funeral.

Knowing that the death of their son had put a tremendous strain on their marriage, Cathy persuaded her husband to go to meetings of Compassionate Friends, a group for parents whose children have died. Encouraged by those who had experienced similar pain, Cathy and

her husband began to communicate more honestly, and their relationship became a source of
comfort for them both.

Take a few moments to imagine yourself as a
plant or flower. Closing your eyes, see or sense
the garden or pot in which you are planted.
What do you, as a plant, want and need more or
less of? How can you provide that for yourself?

We deserve the support and nurturance of
our own private spot in the sun. When we have
been torn from it, we have the strength and wisdom to re-pot ourselves in a way that allows us
to heal, while anchoring our roots firmly in new
circumstances.

I trust in my ability to heal.

*I nurture and protect myself when my roots
are exposed.*

I turn my face to the sun.

Surviving Soul's Night

NIGHT BLURS THE REVEALING CORNERS of day, obscuring the familiar pegs upon which we hang our facades. Stoic masks dissolve as our most fundamental fears parade in the darkness. Stripped of day's bright distractions, night finds us alone, its black mirror reflecting and magnifying our deepest concerns. In the profound shadows of night we must prepare for the apocalypse horses of isolation and despair that can drag us from our daytime strength into a pit of relentless anxiety and self-pity.

Ironically, sleep—healer and welcome friend to the bereaved—often eludes us in the inky hush of the early morning hours, leaving us unable to suppress the rattle of our shattered hearts. What courage it takes to allow our protective shell of denial to fall away and expose our raw vulnerabilities to the stark truth of sleepless darkness. Yet we need to prepare ourselves to face the anguish of those hours and experience the pain that allows healing to go forward.

If you find yourself in need of surviving midnight anxiety, make a survival kit for yourself before you go to bed. Having done so, you will have an option if sleeplessness persists. Perhaps creating a sanctuary, a welcoming retreat filled with belongings that bring you solace, where you can go for succor will be comforting. Lighting candles, listening to inspirational or soothing tapes, writing in a journal, praying—all of these can be conducive to quieting our souls in the tremulous loneliness of a sleepless night. But *you* know best what can bring consolation to you.

If fear is a night child, so are faith and hope. In the deep velvet of silence the Comforter can draw near and hold us in an unfailing embrace. Into the very midst of our worst night terrors often comes a Light Bearer, assuring us that we are loved and protected.

Outer darkness invites us to seek the light within and welcome the visiting Comforter who bears peace of mind in one hand and assurance in the other.

❦

*Even when I am unable to feel the presence,
I know that God is with me.*

*I courageously move through my night terrors
toward healing.*

I am safe. I am protected. I am loved.

Trusting the
Feminine Within

*To live is so startling it leaves little time
for anything else.*

—*Emily Dickinson*

BIRTH IS A MIRACULOUS AFFIRMATION of our ability to trust the feminine. Don't women, after all, have the awe-inspiring power to accept and incorporate the masculine and, together, create life? I believe that fear of this wondrous power is at the root of our distrust of the feminine. What a responsibility to accept and support such power.

Even if we never give birth to a child, we regularly and naturally conceive, nurture, and birth life in ourselves and others through emotional support and love. Realizing that we carry the power and innate wisdom to generate spiritual, emotional, and physical life, we can have confidence in the feminine within, knowing that she is willing and able to create a balanced and harmonious life for us when we choose to listen to her perceptive counsel.

The Sacred Feminine, in her highest reality, embraces all, synthesizing the divergent and the similar, welcoming both the wounded and the wise to her breast. She honors the Whole and is wholly trustworthy.

Honoring the Feminine Way

WATER, THE MOST POWERFUL *AND* MOST
yielding of the elements, symbolizes the feminine way: strong and never deterred from its
goal of union with its source, yet adaptable and
creative as to the means by which it arrives at
its destination. The feminine way is the way of
the heart, unfolding and blooming in concert
with the natural flow of life.

I learned a meaningful lesson about honoring
the feminine way from the actor Gary Busey.
While rewinding my aerobics tape, I inadver-
tently tuned in to a television interview just in
time to hear him discuss his near death experience following a motorcycle accident. In a
sincere and soft-spoken way, Gary described
seeing an incredibly beautiful light from which
three androgynous Beings lovingly told him
that the greatest tragedy was not death but
what dies in us as we live. When asked by
the clearly skeptical interviewer how he had
changed, Gary said, "I'm more process oriented—not so goal oriented—and I see more
into the heart of people and situations." "Are
you happier?" she inquired. "Absolutely! Defi-

nitely! No comparison!" was his immediate response.

In other words, Gary Busey was catapulted off his motorcycle into an experience in which he learned to honor his feminine nature. I was impressed by how self-confident and peaceful he appeared as a result.

Visualize yourself as water, strong and powerful yet yielding and adaptable. Explore where you are now and where you want to go as this body of water. Absorb the feminine attributes of the water until you feel as though you have become one with it. Relax in the awareness that, while there may be temporary dams, *nothing* permanently impedes your journey toward eventual union with your source. If the water you imagine doesn't feel right—either too powerful, meandering, frozen, or stagnant—change it. Envision exactly what you yearn for from your feminine way. What "water-ness" do you want to bring into your daily life to better express your femininity?

I honor and respect my femininity.
I am able to be strong and flexible.
I trust my ability to flow with life.

Discovering the
Sand Dollar's Surprise

WHEN WE SHAKE AN INTACT SAND DOLLAR, we can hear a little rattle and know that some surprise remains hidden inside. Breaking open the shell reveals five delicate objects resembling doves or angels. If Mother Nature unfailingly endows the simple sand dollar with angels, can we not trust that she does the same with us?

Although the sand dollar is pretty when whole, it's even more miraculous when broken and able to share its surprise. That's a lot like us; although we may look good and function well, it often takes breaking free of old patterns for us to really uncover the marvels within us.

To facilitate the process of discovering our hidden treasures, we need to examine the areas around which we have built protective shells and uncover the fears that prompted our need for shielding. For instance, out of a fear of rejection, I used to hide my opinions if they disagreed with others'. Another woman I know camouflages her sensitivity and vulnerability with a smoke screen of caustic humor.

To help you break free, make a list of ways in which you protect yourself. What shells do you hide in? Following that, write a separate list of the fears that originally made you feel the need for protection. Choose one fear to concentrate on now, and gently close your eyes. Allow a picture of the woman or girl within, who holds that fear, to come into your mind's eye. As much as you can, accept and befriend her. If that's difficult, just be with her, asking that your acceptance of her grow each day. Over time, repeat this meditation with the other fears that have confined you, for by accepting the wounded parts of ourselves, we begin to melt their defenses.

We are all laden with gifts and talents yearning to be released in order for their blessings to fly free.

I am free to be authentically me.

I know that I have many gifts and talents to share.

Reawakening to Wonder

HOW CONSCIOUS AND AWAKE ARE WE?
Do we savor the current moment or squander it
in anticipation or dread of tomorrow? One of
the reasons children are so good for us is that
they remind us to be absolutely present in the
here and now. Taking a walk with a small child
reeducates us in the ability to give wonder-filled
attention to whatever we focus on.

The feminine within resonates to the same
miraculous music that children do. It loves
beauty and relationships, and savors genuine
connections with people, things, and experiences. Reawakening to wonder reconnects us to
the childlike attributes of attention and appreciation. Events and feelings become special and
sacred when framed in undivided attention. Life
becomes a fully conscious experience when
made up of moments when we are really *real* and
truly *present.*

As an experiment in reawakening to wonder,
imagine that you are three or four years old and
explore your yard or a park for half an hour. If
the weather doesn't permit outdoor exploration,
take a toddler-walk around your own home. Pay
attention to the textures and tidbits; feel and

even taste objects so familiar that you may not have really seen them since you last dusted, if even then. Open completely to the moment and the adventures it presents. *Awake* to your surroundings. Lose yourself in the here and now. Encourage yourself to be *amazed* and awed by the simplest flower or bug. Close your eyes and "see" objects with your other senses. Enjoy and relish what your childlike feminine self longs to appreciate more often.

When we realize that life is too precious to sleep through and accept our need to make time for the magical minutiae, we will be honoring the feminine within and supporting our much neglected inner child's desire to be awake to wonder. All of life, even the difficulties, can more readily be perceived as miraculous and wonderful when we encourage ourselves to become wonder-full.

I stop and take time to appreciate life's little wonders.

I invite my wonder-filled inner child out to play.

Inviting Spirit Through

SPIRIT NEEDS US. WE ARE THE OPENINGS through which She can express. As we dismantle our own roadblocks toward spirituality, we can become Spirit's avenues and freeways (as well as back roads and dogtrots), her messengers of love and acceptance.

Although it may seem paradoxical, one of the biggest obstacles blocking Spirit from working through us is our own lack of self-love. Spirit can move only through a channel that, at some deep level, knows itself worthy and capable of such a mission.

The feminine within bears an intuitive flame that illumines awareness of our innate worthiness. Only as we come to listen to our wise feminine nature can we accept Spirit's commission to use us as a gateway for good.

Relax in a comfortable, quiet place where you will not be disturbed. For the first few minutes concentrate on your breathing, using as a prayer or mantra the words *opening* as you inhale and *to spirit* as you exhale. Very gently visualize a serene environment that you intuitively know is a place of sacred learning for you. Then confidently, without undue effort, invite a symbol of Spirit to join you. If you don't feel totally comfortable with the image that appears, it's not the appropriate one. Have it vanish, and ask for the right symbol to emerge.

When you are satisfied with your symbol, rest in its presence. Soak in its unconditional love. As you become more trusting of your Spirit, present to it one of the more shadowy sides of yourself, a part that shames or irritates you. Allow Spirit to minister to this dark aspect, bathing it in the light of unconditional recognition. As much as you can, open up to seeing the good buried in this aspect of yourself and, thereby, facilitate its transformation. Then bid goodbye to your Spirit, knowing that She is always available to you.

We are facets of the Whole, splinters of the Divine, through which the light of Spirit longs to shine.

I am worthy of allowing Spirit to flow through me.

I am a facet of the Divine through which loves flows.

Owning Our Inheritance

WE ARE DAUGHTERS OF LIFE'S GENEROSITY, constantly surrounded by the altruism of Mother Earth and the myriad blessings present in work and relationships. It is our birthright to joyously claim this bountiful inheritance. Katherine Mansfield summed up her appreciative attitude beautifully when she said, "Life never becomes a habit to me. It's always a marvel."

One of the major keys to owning our legacy of good is to first appreciate all that we have and are privileged to enjoy now. Because feminine nature excels at appreciation, once we focus our attention in that direction, we can trust that it will flow naturally.

Of course there will always be difficult and painful things that we don't appreciate, but if we become so absorbed in them that we're blind to our blessings, our inheritance remains unclaimed and our lives seem gray and impoverished. Unlike sponges, we are in charge of what we soak up. We can choose to saturate ourselves with "Ain't it awful!" or we can overflow with gratitude and appreciation. Concentrating on the gold nuggets life offers, rather than the lumps of coal, gives us the feeling of being a beloved child, not an abandoned orphan.

Gently and without judgment, examine your outlook. Honestly take stock of your attitude. Is life a marvel or a hassle? Do you see the dust in a shaft of sunlight or feel its warmth? Are most people friendly and accepting, or are they out to get you? Do you appreciate your inheritance—all the varied physical, emotional, mental, and spiritual affluence—by counting your blessings, or do you reject it by centering on your *mis*fortunes?

Take a moment to visualize yourself in a beautiful gallery and begin to fill it with a display of your personal blessings. Maybe your array will include supportive relationships, good health, spiritual beliefs, satisfying work, gorgeous flowers, favorite books, uplifting ideas, peace of mind, and trust in yourself. As you carefully create your treasure trove, do so with thankful appreciation for your vast inheritance.

❧

Life is always a marvel to me.
I am thankful for Life's gifts.

Wising Up

IT'S TRUE THAT WISDOM COMES FROM making mistakes and learning from them. The try-fail-succeed triune certainly does encourage us to increase our understanding of what is true, right, and lasting; but we also have an innate wisdom that we often fail to trust. One of the most powerful ways we can wise up is to acknowledge and act on that small, sagacious voice within.

It has taken me a long time to trust my own inner wisdom, and a large part of my journey toward self-love has included learning to listen and forgiving myself for not always honoring what I intuitively *knew*. One of my most dramatic denials came as I was walking down the aisle on my first wedding day. An interior sage was warning, "This is not right . . . I don't know why, but I know it isn't." I spent the next twelve years doing everything humanly possible to prove myself wrong, but we divorced anyway. I had *known*, but I had not listened.

Take a few self-supportive minutes to sit in a comfortable place and gently close your eyes. In concert with your breath, repeat the simple but profound sentence: I know. Continue this for a few minutes. If you notice you're thinking something else, easily return to *I know*.

In the landscape of your mind, see yourself in a lush meadow at the base of a mountain. Enjoy the sights and smells until the sound of water draws you up the mountainside. After an effortless climb you reach a level spot where a clear, steady spring is flowing from the mountain into a crystal pool. Feeling comfortable and at home there, stop and savor the freshness of the air and water. Drink from the spring, and as you do, realize that within you is a comparable fountain of wisdom. Ever flowing, ever clear, ever wise. Accept the awareness of your well-spring of wisdom, honoring it through trust.

We know! As we have the courage to open to and sincerely trust our feminine within, *woman* and *wise* will become synonymous—a matched set.

I trust my inner wisdom.

Each day I am more aware of my inner sage.

Reclaiming the Crone

PROBABLY OUR ANCIENT ANCESTORS were much more sanguine about aging than we are because they revered the virtues that come with years and experience. Such cultures divided female development into three phases: maiden, mother, and crone.

The crone was wisdom personified. Ancient people saw, in woman's ability to bear children, their own bond to the sacred cycle of life and death. They believed that a woman withheld her menstrual blood to create a baby—life. As her menses stopped with the onset of menopause, they believed that a woman now held back the menstrual blood to birth wisdom. The crone's task was to embrace her wisdom, expand her creativity, and share, especially with other women, the knowledge she had gleaned from her years of experience.

Our foremothers and fathers respected crones and relied upon their counsel and guidance. Following their lead, we need to reclaim that respect *within* ourselves. When we can accept and respect our own creativity and wisdom on a deep level, others will naturally begin to view us as worthy of respect.

Turning fifty was a huge milestone for me. I committed myself to the belief that I had at least one foot in the Wisdom Ring; and when I slip into doubt, as I still do of course, I try to quickly remind myself of my years of experience and my commitment to owning my own excellence. If I can't sustain support for myself, I call in the cavalry by talking to friends who I know believe in me *and* are also dedicated to reclaiming their crone. As a lighthearted reminder, I have cards tacked around the house that say, *Caution, Crone Crossing!*

It's been said that in youth we learn and in age we understand. We can mine the gold of our years of experience by trusting that we have a vast storehouse of wisdom which we are invited to share with others. With that understanding will come the reclamation of our crone, in her highest form.

I embrace my wisdom and share it with others.

I respect myself and the wisdom I have gleaned from experience.

Completing the Circle

WE WOMEN CARRY THE FEMININE energy of the world. It is our task to honor the feminine in ourselves and insist it be honored in others and by others. We need to welcome, as our sacred duty, the task of bringing forth, from the shadows of obscurity, the feminine principles of kindness, consideration, and reverence in our personal lives and on our planet, so that we all can move from competition and chaos to cooperation and compassion.

It is our calling to complete the sacred circle of support by accepting blessings and *becoming* a blessing. Culturally and socially we have been trained to give to others, but in order to be an integral and constructive cog in the wheel of life, we must first complete the sacred circle within ourselves—feeding *ourselves* the feminine fruits of kindness, consideration, and reverence. From a vessel filled with such fruits, we'll be able to freely pour our best into the Whole, giving God and Her children the bountiful harvest of our love.

Because preparing ourselves to complete the circle is a sacred charge, reverently ask yourself what kind of blessing you would like to become. Are you already blessing *yourself* in that way? If not, what do you need to do in order to complete your inner circle? What attitudes would you like to change about yourself? What wounds need healing? What compassion do you need to show yourself? What fruits do you need to trustfully place in your vessel?

Like a pebble tossed in a pond, as we complete our inner circle by becoming a blessing to ourselves, circles of blessings will emanate from us to include countless others.

❦

I give to myself as I give to others.

In all ways I seek to be a blessing.

I am an essential part of the blessed circle of giving and receiving.

Embracing the Consort

HARMONY IN OUR LIVES IS SOMETHING we all yearn for and work toward. But for this to happen we must first balance our dual inner nature, creating an intimate partnership of equals between the feminine and masculine energies in us—a sacred marriage that gives birth to the whole person.

Because society has enshrined the masculine by declaring it the *right* way to be in our world, we may first need to dethrone our masculine energy by empowering and honoring our feminine within, encouraging her to be our most potent inner influence. When we're strong enough to embrace, but not be overwhelmed by, our left-brain consort of male energy, femininity and masculinity can share the throne of our hearts, generating a synthesis between the differing, but equally valuable, aspects of our beings.

Barbara, an incest survivor, was having difficulty balancing her masculine and feminine energies. She vacillated between living totally in her feelings and being stoically rigid and controlling. It was an emotional roller coaster that caused her both emotional and practical difficulties. A series of dreams in which she gave birth to baby boys and felt unbounded love as she nursed and nurtured them helped Barbara heal the fear of men that she carried from her childhood trauma.

Through the dreams presented by her wise subconscious, Barbara realized that there was a deep part of her that was untouched by her frightening experiences with men, an aspect of herself that welcomed and trusted both the masculine and feminine energies. From that base of inner awareness, Barbara began to balance and harmonize her masculine and feminine within.

Like Barbara, we can tune in to our male and female selves and bring them into balance. Calling up and listening to the masculine and feminine aspects of ourselves lets us know if we have resistance to either energy. If there is quite a bit, I strongly suggest you find a therapist or friend who can help you trust and accept both the queen and the consort within.

❧

I embrace my masculine energy with love and acceptance.

I am balanced and harmonized within myself.

Respecting Our Initiations

AT LEAST TWO ELEMENTS ARE ALWAYS present in initiation rites: an emotional and/or physical challenge, and the summons to let go of the old and move into the new. Because our psyches naturally move toward growth and wholeness, we constantly support our evolution by inviting initiation into our lives, whether we are conscious of doing so or not. Moving out on our own, making a living, falling in love, getting married, having a baby, being ill or caring for someone who is ill, surviving the death of someone we love are all initiations that both wound and renew us. Each of these initiations asks us to change, evolve, mature, grow up, and become the best that we can be.

If we're dragged kicking and screaming to an initiation, viewing it as an arbitrary happening over which we have no power, we've probably misunderstood our innate drive toward wholeness and will undoubtedly miss the invaluable learning intrinsic in it.

None of us eagerly hails growth that entails emotional or physical pain, but viewing our initiations as opportunities to become a wiser and more compassionate woman helps us feel less like victims and more like students. Being committed to learning as much as we can in our lifetime allows us to become a wounded healer whose empathy and understanding are the foundation of her healing energy. Perceiving our initiations as sacred rites of passage into the next dimension of our development helps us understand that from the blood of our initiation wounds can flow increased compassion, wisdom, and personal empowerment.

Trusting our innate wisdom, especially in the face of difficult initiations that rip us from people or circumstances we love, is a very powerful and necessary way to emotionally support ourselves. Opening to *all* of life's experiences empowers our intuition to become a wise inner sovereign, choosing well what lessons we learn.

Respecting our initiations and trusting the teachings that they bestow will bring us into communion with the collective wisdom and closer to wholeness within ourselves.

I accept and learn from the initiations life presents.
I trust myself to grow through the pain of initiation.

Gathering the Harvest
of Maturity

THERE ARE MANY BLESSINGS TO BE harvested as we mature and ripen within ourselves: peace of mind, flexibility, trust, and acceptance, to name a few. As we develop, we often come into our own power and stop spending time, energy, and money on things that no longer satisfy us. Carl Jung, the eminent Swiss psychologist, believed that our natural ability to do what we choose rather than what we're told to do strongly emerges during maturity, often after being *sub*merged for many years. What a harvest that could be.

Although age is not the only determining factor, the myriad experiences we have as a result of aging do offer us many chances to ripen into maturity. I have heard it said that when Sleeping Beauty wakes up she is almost fifty years old. The writer M.C. Richards has a wonderful view on Sleeping Beauty's wake-up call: "The old saying that life begins at forty has its basis in fact. For in maturity occurs a natural birth of a selfhood which has been growing within the womb of spirit. The generative principle never ceases. It was a long time before I felt reborn within myself the intuitions natural to childhood, when freedom is a loyalty to life."

Freedom is a loyalty to life. What a profound observation. And who could be better at being loyal to life than women, who actually have the capacity to birth life from their own bodies? The feminine within all women is aware of the cycle of life at a primal and cellular level. We *know;* we *wait;* we *trust.* We are attuned to the earth, moon, and sun because of our own cyclic nature, just as Mother Nature is attuned to her own sowing, growing, and harvesting cycle. What a natural jump for us, then, to become attuned to and grateful for the aging cycle of our life that brings with it increased freedom and maturity.

I happily gather the harvest of my maturity.

I am productive now.

I choose to do what feels right for me.

Leaving White Space

WHEN WE OPEN OUR DAILY CALENDARS, how much white space do we see? Do we have blocks of unscheduled time or is our calendar filled to overflowing with commitments, committees, and appointments? Without white space in which to relax and be, we become overstimulated and sometimes even addicted to intensity—like a shark, constantly moving even in sleep.

We women have the abilities of a master juggler. We can survive while keeping a heroic number of balls in the air, but do we really thrive while doing so? Yes, if we also make room for plenty of silence in which meaning and wisdom can truly bloom. Blessings flow to us when nurtured in refreshing solitude.

Solitude gives us the opportunity to know what we feel and know what we know. Anne Morrow Lindbergh underscores that thought in *Gift from the Sea* when she says, "For it is only framed in space that beauty blooms. Only in space are events and objects and people unique and significant—and therefore beautiful."

In order to grow emotionally and spiritually, we must make white space a priority. It is in the privacy of white space that our hearts heal and expand. In the quiet of white space we can hear the urgings of our higher selves and receive the mysterious teachings from the feminine within. Framing our lives with intervals of contemplation and solitude gives us a better sense of self and greater peace of mind. Bringing these attributes into our daily life blesses not only ourselves but also those with whom we relate.

As an experiment, give yourself permission to take ten minutes a day just for you—ten minutes of solitude and silence. Make no demands upon yourself about how to "use" the time; just relax and be quiet. As you can, extend your solitary times. Although other time demands will be noisier, give yourself the spirit-enhancing gift of listening to the call from your higher self for white space, and rest and become revitalized in the silence. We can reap the benefits of solitude now.

I leave white space just for me.

I rest in the silence.

I give myself permission to reap the blessings of solitude.

Transforming Archetypal Fears

WE WOMEN ARE QUESTING FOR A definition of the feminine that's relevant for us today. In our search, we're reviewing how the feminine has been viewed in the past, and we are uprooting individual and collective fears about what it might mean for us to truly energize and utilize our feminine power.

Many of our fears are grounded in fact. Historians tell us that in the three years of the Spanish Inquisition nine million women were burned as witches. Later, in our own country, the same fate befell many women in New England. In general, these gender holocausts were perpetrated against women who were sought after for their healing, counseling, and midwifery skills. Their knowledge and wisdom—and in some cases, eccentricity—was perceived as a threat to the "powers that be" and so they were destroyed.

Is it any wonder that we hesitate to trust and empower our feminine nature? Embedded in our history are two messages: *wisdom is punishable by death, and to be fully empowered is to be life-threateningly vulnerable.* Our subconscious response to this is often fear of bucking the establishment, whether the establishment is the men in our lives, our bosses, our government, or even our own children.

What the executioners began with their witch burnings, we have perpetuated through our unexamined personal and archetypal fears. We are changing that, but we still need to transform any ancient fears that continue to lurk in the shadows of our subconscious. Only by bringing these fears into the light, where they can be examined for their present-day validity, will we transform them.

I free myself from ancient and archetypal fears by examining and transforming them.

I am safe and protected.

I am wise and empowered.

Welcoming Our Angels

WRESTLING WITH OUR DEMONS IS SIMPLE and often feels more appropriate than embracing our angels. We seem determined to invite into the ring of our life the demons of self-deprecation and disbelief, allowing them to throw us to the mat with alarming regularity. It's a different story when our angels—such as wisdom and intuition—come calling. We can't believe that they are real or that we are worthy of entertaining them.

One of the main reasons it's so much easier to acknowledge our demons is that we've been taught to trust them. Other people will affirm their existence with such statements as, "That's a dumb idea!" or "You're crazy." We learn to accept that we're not smart or worthwhile, and we then welcome representatives of our lower selves, our demons, into our belief systems because of their familiarity.

Angels, on the other hand, are emissaries of our higher selves, the essence of our beings, a distillation of our experience and innate knowledge. They are real, and we need to give ourselves the gift of learning to accept and trust their presence instead of denying and wrestling with them each time they appear.

Allow yourself to become quiet and centered, stilling your mind to the best of your ability. Imagine that you are seated in the midst of a soft, warm light. Feel it being absorbed into your body and your being. At the edge of the light stands an angel of intuition as well as a demon of self-doubt. Familiarize yourself with both of these visitors and then firmly insist that self-doubt fade away. Summon your angel of intuition to share the warmth and softness of the light with you. Open yourself in welcome to this symbol of your intuitive inner femininity.

We owe it to ourselves and those with whom we're in relationship to honor the wise and wonderful feminine within by accepting the aspects of our higher selves and acting in accordance with their principles.

I encourage myself to believe in my higher qualities.

*I welcome my angels of intuition and
wisdom into my awareness.*

I am wise.

Wielding Soft Power

I FIRST HEARD THE TERM *SOFT POWER* from a wise young herbalist who is a scholar of the feminine mysteries. Although she often works ceremonially with young girls about to begin their menses, I met Gina at a fiftieth birthday celebration where she led us in blessing this woman's transition from mother to crone. I was touched by Gina's message of the potency, grace, wisdom, and responsibility of owning our feminine power in its highest form.

True feminine power is soft, meant to feed and heal ourselves, others, and our planet. I am reminded of our breasts with which we comfort and feed our children. Ideally we, ourselves, are like breasts—soft yet strong, beautiful and miraculous, able to provide pleasure as well as sustenance. As we women move from the discomfort of denying and being denied our personal power, to the supportive place of accepting and using it, we need to hold the highest conception of this power forever at the forefront of our minds.

Find a candle that symbolizes the feminine to you. At a time when you are confident of not being disturbed, light your candle and concentrate on the flame. As you rest in the glow, invite into your circle of light a female symbol for your feminine power in its highest expression.

If the symbol that first appears doesn't feel loving and supportive, invite it to leave. Once again focus on your candle flame and, when you feel ready, issue the invitation again. Become acquainted with the symbol of your feminine power, and bask in her wisdom. Ask her help in consistently and lovingly wielding your genuine, soft power. At the completion of your time together, she has a gift for you. Accept it with the full awareness that you are worthy of receiving it. Hold her gift, as a blessing and affirmation of your own soft empowerment, close to your heart.

Remember a woman's power is restorative, not destructive. With genuine feminine power, we can rebuild, replenish, and renew that which has been depleted.

I accept and embrace my soft feminine power.
I dedicate my power to the expansion of love.

Lighting Our Flame

WHILE MEDITATING ON THE FLAME OF a candle floating in an iridescent, crystal wine glass, I was struck by the similarity of this candle to the potential we all have floating within us. Spiritual promise, our own unique light source, lies waiting to catch fire. We hold the matches, and it's our choice whether we light our interior candle or leave it floating coolly in the shadows.

Our spiritual potential will wait, for it is eternal. But would we not be warmer and happier—more our authentic selves—if we moved through the necessities, joys, and sorrows of our days warmed by the glow of this inner fire?

While contemplating the floating candle, one important thing I noticed was that the imperfections in the crystal showed up more clearly when the candle was burning than they did when it was cold. Maybe the defects amplified by the candlelight are symbolic of the fact that, even when we ignite our flame and consciously travel the path to enlightenment, we will not be perfect. Nor do we need to be. *But,* by lighting our inner flame, we *will* cast out darkness.

Settle in a comfortable, dark place and light a candle, quietly observing how far the light from this single candle travels. Notice the softness of objects illumined by it. As your breath deepens, gently allow your eyes to float closed. Without effort imagine yourself seated in front of a small bonfire. Well-being permeates your senses as you feel the warmth from the crackling flames. Looking down you see an exquisite candle lying on a velvet cloak and you intuitively know that these gifts are for you. Lighting the candle from the original fire, wrap yourself securely in the cloak and allow yourself to rest there, being renewed by your magical candle. When it feels appropriate to you, gently and carefully return to the present, knowing that the flame you carry is eternal.

Consciously lighting our spiritual flame means that we can more genuinely provide the warmth and comfort of illumined love both to ourselves and others.

❦

I am a spiritual being.
I have a radiant inner life.

Seeing the Friendly
Face of God

HOW MANY OF US, AS LITTLE GIRLS, believed that God was a man? Well, that may have been okay if all the men we knew were loving and kind, but if they were not, our view of God was diminished and tainted. I don't pretend to really *know* what God is like, but my heart resonates with the idea that God is way too immense for us to possibly imagine. I believe that God incorporates all the wonderful qualities inherent in both women and men, as well as countless other attributes beyond our capacity to understand.

I wonder if God really cares how we view Her/Him/It as long as the face we turn to for comfort, love, and guidance is a *friendly* one. I like to believe that God wishes we felt able to safely and trustingly rest in Its Divine, Mysterious Presence.

Our need for spiritual connection is greater, even, than our need for interpersonal connection. But we can unite at a heart level with only a loving and friendly God, not a fearful one. Give yourself the priceless gift of exploring your current relationship to God. If your connection with the Divine is close, loving, and friendly, that's wonderful, and I'm sure your life is an inspirational light to others. But, if you'd like to see a friendlier face when you think of God, begin by exploring your most firmly held inner beliefs. Do you feel worthy of loving attention from God? Do you fear or resist the idea of a God? When you try to conjure up an image of God, what does it look like? What would it take for you and God to be *friends*?

The friendliest face of God lives in our inner temple of genuine self-love and acceptance. When we can befriend ourselves, we will more than likely be able to let God befriend us, also. From that sacred space, God can move through us and, in grace, bless all those who cross our path.

I am worthy of God's love.
I invite God to work through me.
God is love, and so am I.

Personal Note

Thank you for reading THE WOMAN'S BOOK OF CONFIDENCE. I believe we're all on a very important journey toward true valuation of women and the feminine values and ideals, and I appreciate us traveling a similar path via these ideas and meditations. Together, we are stronger and can soar more easily toward our unique, personal destiny, and reach out to support others without draining ourselves in the process.

If you have ideas or experiences you would like to share, or if you would like to purchase signed copies of THE WOMAN'S BOOK OF CONFIDENCE, THE COURAGE TO BE YOURSELF, THE WOMAN'S BOOK OF COURAGE, AUTUMN OF THE SPRING CHICKEN, or HEART CENTERED MARRIAGE please write to me:

> Sue Patton Thoele
> P.O. Box 1519
> Boulder, CO 80306-1519

Sue Patton Thoele

Sue Patton Thoele was a psychotherapist for twenty years, but is now concentrating on her passion for writing. She and her husband, Gene, live in Boulder, Colorado, and have four adult children and one grandchild.